Tales from the Peoli Road

Wit and humor of very real people,
who just happen to be Amish.

Eli R. Beachy

HERALD PRESS
Scottdale, Pennsylvania
Waterloo, Ontario

Library of Congress Cataloging-in-Publication Data
Beachy, Eli R., 1950-
   Tales from the Peoli Road / Eli R. Beachy.
      p. cm.
   ISBN 0-8361-3578-4
   1. Amish—Ohio—Social life and customs—Anecdotes. 2. Amish—
Ohio—Social life and customs—Humor. I. Title.
F550.M45B42 1992
977.1'0088287—dc20   91-37263
                                                          CIP

The paper used in this publication is recycled and meets the minimum
requirements of American National Standard for Information
Sciences—Permanence of Paper for Printed Library Materials, ANSI
Z39.48-1984.

To Punkin

His ... even-balanced soul ...
Business could not make dull,
nor passion wild:
Who saw life steadily and saw it whole.

—Matthew Arnold

Contents

Foreword

When Eli stopped by the mill with a copy of his writing, I was considerably interested. Perhaps I was even flattered a bit when he asked me to pen a few lines of foreword. Not being much for letters, I had trouble writing my piece until I decided to make honesty the best policy.

I would say these tales will be quite popular around here, not for the content, but for each of the loafers to see if he's been included. Upon reading the text, I would imagine most will agree with me that Eli did take a liberty or two on a few details. Not to say he'd lie or anything, but Eli does tend to have an imagination.

An imagination is one thing the reader won't need if he comes looking to find out about Amish life. It's well spelled out for our neck of the woods. After seeing so much in print that just isn't true, it's nice to read something you can believe, for the most part, about things here in Ohio.

There's no sense in picking on the small points. A text like this is long overdue. Oftentimes I've wondered if some of these self-appointed experts on the Amish ever held the business end of a cow. Printing a book like this won't end all the stupidity, but it is a step in the right direction.

That's about all I care to say, I suppose. If I write any more, I'll get to editorializing, and I'm no newspaper man.

I'll just leave it to you to form your own opinions on what we know is true.

Best of luck to you until we see you along the Peoli Road.

Yours,

Jaeky A. Miller

Jake A. Miller
On the Peoli Road

Preface

The Amish have been Ohioans since 1809, yet few of the world know any more of the Plain People today than in pioneer times. My stories come out of a society veiled by misperceptions of onlooking curiosity seekers. They present a uniquely Amish view on the world.

Here you will find humorous and enlightening exploits and misadventures of those very real people who happen to be Amish. From the excited father-to-be who rushes off to the hospital without his expectant wife, to the shrewd manipulations of a somewhat underhanded carpenter crew, the humanity of the Plain People comes through.

In the Amish world, devoid of television and even electricity, storytelling remains a favorite form of entertainment. These tales have amused the loafers at many a horse sale, social gathering, or wherever two or more visit. A name or two has been changed to protect the guilty, or sometimes not, to keep my readers guessing. But every event really did occur, whether some care to admit it or not.

As the modern world speeds by in a never-ending race to somewhere, three facts will remain. There will always be an Amish Ohio, there will always be one more story to tell about it, and life will go on, even down the Peoli Road.

—Eli R. Beachy, once a carpenter, now an author

1

Doctoring

The Amish are genetically bred to be cheap.
—Eli R. Beachy

You might call it odd that an entire road full of people can live without electricity today, in the 1990s. Another might say it is peculiar that those same folk can also get by quite well without the automobile. Even more might be dumbfounded to learn that there are some without indoor plumbing. When we see that back home, down the Peoli Road, we call it *unser Leit,* our people. When you see it, you call it *the Amish.*

It strikes folks strange down our way that the Amish have become the third largest tourist attraction in Ohio these days. Two big, multimillion-dollar amusement parks come first, and then the Peoli People. To be honest with you, it makes no sense to us. We've been living our own life our own way without too much help all these years. Now, within the last ten years, all sorts of people come running into what Ohio calls Amish Country like they're trying to find something.

Maybe it's more because they forgot some things than that they're looking to find new thoughts. Everything the Amish are doing today in their living is the way all of rural

America was doing things ninety years ago. If those visitors are coming to look for something spiritual, they sure have a roundabout way of finding that, too. All they'd have to do is ask. But city people have a tendency to be a bit strange, anyway.

Once I was to Cleveland. I'll tell you, it's as bad as Millersburg on a Saturday. People rushing here and there, all seeming to be looking for some sort of excitement. We don't need the big city for wild times. Around here, at least, it all started three years ago one New Year's Eve.

An hour or so before dark, half a dozen of us had congregated down at the mill, holding what we call our New Year's Eve Gala. It was crisp, but not winter cold yet that year. Actually, with the exception of substituting my black felt for the summer straw hat, I think I was wearing the exact same clothes I was wearing the beginning of September.

Our crowd that had collected likes to consider ourselves the trustees of the Peoli Road, the wise ones and all, but the womenfolk much prefer to brand us for what we are, the loafers. At any rate, we were all standing there, sipping on a little of the homemade root beer that Moses likes to brew up. All of a sudden, running down the road, here came Ivan. He was running so fast, I was afraid the house was on fire.

"No, no," he managed to gasp out, "it's my wife. The little one's on the way!"

As we watched him, we all started grinning, thinking of a new arrival in our community. The big, burly redhead ran over to the phone booth to call Joe, a local fellow who liked to drive for the Amish. You may have heard that the Plain People don't go for having a telephone, and that's

true, but there's nothing wrong with its proper use. Same with the automobile. We wouldn't want to own one, but when need be, a ride can be quite handy.

Sure enough, in just a few minutes, here came Joe in his old blue Ford pickup. He and Ivan talked, Ivan jumped in, and off they went, down Old 21 headed for Memorial Hospital.

Such a joyous occasion called for another round of the root beer. We weren't but three or four sips into the mug when here came Joe, racing his Ford up the road past us and right on up the Peoli Road. This was confusing, but trust old Amos to advise patience, and he was right.

In just a few minutes, here came Joe down the road again. This time he was blowing the air horn and hooting and hollering out the window. He was going quick, but not so quick that we couldn't see Ivan sitting there in the cab with a feed sack over his head.

Ivan was hoping that we would have dispersed by the time they got back, or if not, that we wouldn't recognize him, but that wasn't to be. We all instantly grasped the situation and knew that the feed sack wasn't what was important. What the big thing was all about was between Joe and Ivan there in the truck.

It's hard—no, impossible—to have a son when your wife is sitting on the steps of the homeplace up the Peoli Road, wondering what's taking you so long to make that phone call. The expected child turned out to be twin sons, first children born in the county that year at Memorial Hospital.

Sagas like that remind me that there are some who believe the Amish don't take to doctoring. That's a silly thought, there being nothing more precious than human life. The problem comes when we realize the Amish are genetically bred to be cheap, closer to a dollar bill than George Washington. Of us all, there's none as cheap as Old Weaver.

Old Weaver thought it horrible that our doctor hereabouts charged $4.50 for a shot. So Weaver stopped by one day and had the doc show him how to give injections. Weaver left, happy as a clam, whistling through what teeth he had left, and filed that information away in his mind.

As fate would have it, only a few weeks later Mrs. Weaver got to feeling run-down. Old Weaver put two and two together. He knew that when his calves in the barn get run-down, he gives them a shot of vitamin B_{12}. If it's good for the calves, it's got to be good for the wife. Since he knew how to give human injections, that's just what he did, and eventually Mrs. Weaver pepped right up.

It was between the shot and the *eventually* that things

got interesting, though. First thing was, her eyes started to water. Next she swelled up all over. Then she itched and itched. It finally passed, and she felt fine, but there were some tense moments.

A few days later Old Weaver just happened by the doctor's office. Just a hypothetical question, of course, but he wondered what would happen if a man accidentally gave his wife an overdose of, let's say, B_{12}?

Well, the doc is pretty sharp. First thing he said was, "A man don't think much of his spouse to be doing that," and Weaver nods. The doc went on to say how her eyes would water, she'd swell up and itch, but after these symptoms passed, she'd be fine. Then the doctor threw in a little kicker.

"You know, there's a little-known side effect. Ninety-nine times out of one hundred, the lady in question ends up pregnant. You've already got sixteen of your own, don't you, Weaver?"

Weaver started gasping for air, nodded, and went dashing out of the office. Now it could be that Weaver is in that distinct minority. It could be the doc was just pulling his chain a bit. However it worked out, some say there was a very ladylike sigh of relief coming from the Weaver house a couple of weeks later, and the count still stands at sixteen.

2

God's Special Children

Live innocently; God is here.
—Linnaeus

Innocence has nothing to dread.
—Jean Racine

As a young man, I had a chance to experience the benefits of modern medicine myself. Being five, maybe six years of age, I had gotten pretty big for my britches. That bigheadedness got me into problems, and before I was done, I think I caused more trouble than the accidents that had brought people to the hospital in the first place.

We'd been fishing, my family and I. Being a dumb kid, I figured all the biggest fish were out in the center of the lake. The only way my line was going to get there was by casting as far as I could. It didn't matter that my folks were telling me not to do that. With each cast I was trying harder and harder.

In fact, I was casting so hard I even took my hat off for more distance. I cranked back and let go one more time. As the family stood there waiting to see the splash, I realized I had managed to put the fishhook in the back of my head.

Everybody got rather excited about this. I didn't really

hurt and wasn't bleeding or anything. They probably could have worked the hook out right there. But just to be safe, Pop snipped the line and we headed to the hospital.

One of the oldest sports must be the emergency room game. That's where everybody sits around in a small room trying to figure out what's wrong with everybody else. I didn't know anything about it, but the fat woman sitting in the chair next to me must have been an old pro.

When I say fat, I'm understating the situation. She was using all the space possible and then some. She was none too pleased that some squirt of a kid, me, would dare take up a full chair. Since she had everybody else in the room figured out, she started looking us over out of the corner of her eye.

Pop sensed what was going on. Just being a rascal, he said something that made me turn my head to face him. The fat woman got one look at that hook, with the worm still attached, dangling out of my head. She let out a scream and fainted dead away.

With that scene, she got immediate service. Funny, though, how folks preferred to stand rather than fill that empty chair of hers.

However, no amount of medicine or doctors can help some. You may have heard or read that the Amish have in-bred, marrying first cousins as recently as sixty years ago. That may be one of few things you've heard about the Amish that's true. Only now are we seeing the effects. It's difficult to explain other than to tell you about Reuben.

Reuben is a big kid, about six feet, four inches, and 220 pounds, jet black hair and coal-colored eyes. Even though the calendar says he's twenty-four, because of that inbreeding he'll never have any more mind than an eight-

year-old. Work he can, though, and work he does, especially now that his brothers and sisters have grown and started families of their own.

There never was much problem for Reuben to hitch up a team of draft horses, but field work was another matter. Finally, just last year, Reuben's dad decided it was time for him to learn to plow. Time for Reuben to grow one more notch. They hitched the horses to the plow, moved the team over to the field, and got set.

"Now, Reuben, this is what I want," said his dad. "You plow out there to the oak tree, keeping it as straight as you can. It's very simple. Can you do that?"

Reuben nodded, flicked the lines, and off they went. Reuben proceeded to plow a furrow so straight that a surveyor would have been proud. He plowed right out to the oak tree, straight out to the tree, and then he stopped. And stood there. And stood there.

After about five minutes, the old man decided he'd better find out what was wrong. Out across the field he went, worrying and wondering. He got right up beside Reuben and just started to open his mouth when Reuben turned to him and said, "Hi, Poppa. Now what?"

His dad had told him to plow to the tree. He didn't say anything about turning around. When the old man explained about making turns and doing the whole field, it made sense enough to Reuben. Once again he nodded, flicked the lines, and was off.

Troyer was still chuckling about his boy's stunt as I pulled up. We got to visiting, looking at the barn stock, and eating pie while time slipped away. I did want to say hello to Reuben before I left, so Troyer and I headed over to the field.

I can still recall walking up to the gate, hearing Troyer's shriek, and then seeing him run across that freshly plowed field. Oh, yes, every furrow was perfect, as if a master plowman had turned the soil in that field. And then into the next field as well.

Troyer can laugh about it today, but it wasn't funny then. Reuben had plowed the field all right, and since the gate was open, he kept right on going. By the time we got to him, he was three furrows deep into the neighbor's best pasture. Old Weaver's cows were dodging for cover and prime grazing ground was torn to shreds. Things were pretty tense as we worked until well after dark trying to repair the damage by turning the sod back into place. It took us that long to realize one thing: Reuben's dad told him to plow; he never said anything about stopping.

Reuben, and all like him, are what the Amish call God's Special Children. We understand these young ones may be frustrating at times, but they are a pleasant reminder of a state of innocence, too. They will be cherished and cared for until eternity.

Unlike some of our Pennsylvania cousins, Ohio's Amish have not yet started special schools for the disabled. Friends of ours to the north and the west of us, nearer to Berlin, send their special ones to the public training program, and that's good. Round here, in cases like Reuben's, we're more partial to home schooling. That's good, too, but, in a way, Reuben missed out on a most glorious time—school.

3

Schooling

It takes all sorts of in and outdoor schooling
To get adapted to my kind of fooling.
—Robert Frost

When an Amish baby comes into this world, he is a little woodchopper or she is a little dishwasher. The young ones hold that title until about the age of seven. Then, upon entry into the first grade, the young assume a new role, that of scholar.

It was a long struggle for the Amish to establish their own school system. Some point to a 1972 United States Supreme Court case involving the state of Wisconsin and a man named Yoder as a benchmark, but that's not really right. If the truth be known, the words of those justices mirrored what the Ohio Supreme Court had said eleven years before, back in 1961, when they rendered an opinion on a case that began in 1944. That was a long time ago, but we think it was right.

The Amish don't think themselves better than anybody, but they see no need for higher education. The first eight grades are enough, and that's what those jurists said, too. They figured that, even if someone would leave the faith, the skills and the work ethic learned as Amish were so valuable they'd never be a burden on society. Those wise judges have been right up until now, and we'll keep doing out best to prove them right forever.

We've got our own school, Peoli Ridge, with our teacher, Arlene Miller. She's the harnessmaker Mervin's second girl, the one Noah's partial to, but nobody's supposed to know that. This is her second year, and I'd say she enjoys it. Yet there was one day last fall when she had her doubts.

Arlene had read or heard that a good way to increase a scholar's vocabulary is with rhymes. She asked who knew a word that rhymed with *cow*. Up shot a hand, and somebody said, "Mow" (as in *haymow*). That was good, and the next word was *course*. Another hand was up and a student answered, "Horse." One thing for sure, she should have stopped right there.

Teacher wondered if anybody knew a word that sounded like *bird*. Up went little Amos' hand, and he shouted out, "Turd!"

Arlene sent a note home to the Yoder house, but Mrs. Yoder wasn't too hard on Amos. However, I do know that his father, Leroy, is a little more careful about what's said at the supper table these days.

Although I did not go to Peoli Ridge, I can understand situations like this. In my third-grade year, I learned that the way you act at home is not necessarily the way you act in public. At the homeplace, if it itched, you scratched it. I was admonished privately by Teacher that little boys don't scratch that, at least not outside the outhouse.

My start in the educational system would have been traumatic enough for even the bravest of scholars. On the morning of my first day of being a first grader, I received firm instructions in our kitchen. As soon as school was dis-

19

missed that afternoon, I was immediately to run to the swings, sit down, and wait for my sister to walk home with me.

It wasn't necessary for my parents to repeat those instructions, nor did I argue with them as I've seen so many city children do these days. I listened to the words of my parents because I respected and trusted them. They led by example, and I knew if they said for me to do something, it was in my best interest to do it. If they had enough trust in Sis to have her watch out for me, then I knew I could trust her, too. After all, she was a fifth grader.

As hard as I try, I cannot recall a single event of that first day in the classroom itself. Those specifics are lost to my memory completely. The events of the day come into sharp focus only with the tolling of the dismissal bell and my dash to the swings.

Indeed, I did dash right to those swings. I might not have been the first scholar out the door, but no more than three were leading me. With two hops I was on the swing, eagerly awaiting my sister so I could go right home to share my day.

It seemed like the whole school went by me in a solid mass. Even if there were only thirty enrolled in the Glenmont School, all their faces blended together in the congregation of children that swept past me. A few stragglers took a pass or two on the swings, but not for long. No sense in playing if chores were calling. With everybody else gone, I sure did wish that Sis would hurry so we could get home.

I don't know how much time had passed, with me still sitting on that swing. Then Mrs. Weaver came out the school door, headed for home. Teacher lived some distance from the school, so she also drove her buggy even on nice days. The stable some fathers had built for her horse and rig was right near the swings, so it was natural that she'd stroll my way to see what I was up to.

Mrs. Weaver seemed relieved that I wasn't having any problem, that I was just waiting for someone. We talked a bit. She was so nice, and she gave me a lot of encouragement. Being a scholar is no easy task. I was feeling pretty good when she took her leave, hitched up her buggy, and with one last wave, headed for her home. A nice lady, but I wished Sis would hurry with cleaning the blackboards or whatever she was doing.

Even at that young age, I recall that one of my greatest attributes was a vivid imagination. I watched the birds flying over and speculated on what sort of view of earth they must have. The gray squirrel who came close to the swings would soon be holing up for winter in his warm and secure home. I saw myself as a bird in flight and a snuggled squirrel, lost in a most pleasant daydream of a life in nature.

According to the family legend, life went right on that afternoon. Near five that evening, after finishing the work on a chicken coop for neighbor Troyer, Pop came walking up our lane, heading for supper. Through the back door he went, spying the table all set and the meat loaf just coming out of the oven.

Just like every other evening when he came home from work, Dad washed up at the pitcher pump over the sink, asked my mother how her day was, and then announced he was ready to eat. Right after that, when my mother told Sis to call me to supper, the excitement started.

Maybe at first it was more a case of paralysis than excitement. I heard that Sis stopped in her tracks, her face registering first remembrance, then terror. It took a second or two before my mother realized the situation. I'm told her face went that same route. When Dad got the message, they left supper standing and went dashing out the door.

I never realized Dad could be such a fast driver. That buggy was just about on two wheels when they came ripping into the schoolyard that evening. Figuring this meant it was time to go, I finally left my perch on the swing, walked over to the buggy, climbed in, and asked how everybody was, being friendly as I am.

Things were tense that evening. Sis tasted a couple of licks from my mother's strap and then three smacks from Dad's hickory switch. I felt bad about her getting punished, since I had received similar attention in the past, but I also wasn't so dumb as not to savor one benefit of the entire incident.

There never was any worry about me being kidnapped or the like. We figure that God has his eye on little ones around here. The folks weren't worried about me wandering off, either. Even then I was Amish enough to mind my manners and mind my folks even more. No, what ticked off the folks was that by spending all that time sitting on a swing, I hadn't gotten my chores done.

The way they saw it that evening, if Sis didn't feel it necessary that I be home after school, then she could handle my chores for the next week. That notion was so agreeable to me that I decided I'd mention a thought to Sis that evening as she fed the chickens for me. The thought, that anytime she cared to leave me at school was fine with me, only got mentioned once. Sis never said a word or changed expression then or just a minute later, when she jabbed toward my backside with the pitchfork. I jumped! Oh, well, it was worth a try.

In the fifth grade we came in contact with what is known as a school bully. We've always gone for the small, one-room schoolhouse of thirty or so scholars, so it wasn't hard for this bully to unleash a reign of terror. We all fell into line quickly under the most dire threat: if we didn't, we would be "depantsed." So it was a great relief to return to the sixth grade and find the bully had moved on to another area. To be honest, I've often wondered whatever happened to her.

Peoli Ridge is just like all Ohio Amish schools in that it has its own school board. These are fathers who assess the community to keep the school running, pick out the textbooks, and hire the teacher. We've had a problem over the years because our teachers have been younger women. They're Amish, and that's what we want, but they end up getting married and starting a family, changing their own priorities, and rightly so. Things got so desperate before they found Arlene that the school board even asked me to teach a term or two.

One member of the board had been talking to my old teacher from Glenmont, Mrs. Weaver. He misunderstood when she said, as my name was mentioned, that I should have been an astronaut. Since those space jockeys are sharp cookies, the fellows on the board assumed that I must be one, too, and that Mrs. Weaver knew something they didn't.

Fortunately, for all involved, some others checked out this opinion. Indeed, Mrs. Weaver will always believe me to be a good astronaut. After all, when I was in her class all I did was take up space.

Somebody brought the local newspaper for this neck of the woods down to the mill the other day. I'd say there wasn't that much in all those pages of newsprint that I found interesting other than one unusual article. It was a strange way to announce what I'd call some really bad news.

According to the story, the public schools around here gave their scholars a standardized test. The idea was to measure how well the scholars were doing in the basics of education and how much they really knew. At first light, it seemed to be a decent enough notion.

When they got all those tests scored, they found that 48 percent of the scholars had passed the exam. The newspaper explained that meant 48 percent were able to do the minimum level of work acceptable for their grade. They didn't say this, but if 48 percent passed, that says to me that 52 percent failed.

Down the Peoli Road, we don't have the electricity to power all those televisions, radios, or computers. We like to keep everything simple, even the education in our Amish schools. Now it could be that we really miss out by living a life of basics and not having all sorts of extracurricular activities or amusements. We don't have a lot of convenience, but then again, we don't have much failure either.

4

The World of Work

A man can never escape his past.
—Eli R. Beachy

As interesting as school can be for a student, by the age of fourteen and the completion of the eighth grade, it is time to put the books aside. The title of scholar is lost, and the children are now known as the young folks. With head up, it's an all-too-quick march into adulthood via the world of work.

This isn't to say that the Amish children haven't been working before. There's always chores, done with the firm belief that a child who learns to work will never want things handed to him like so many others. It's different now, though. The young folks are learning a trade and, more importantly, earning a dollar or two.

It's a mystery to me where some people get the notion that the Amish are some kind of socialists or something, never chasing after a dollar like everybody else. The Plain People, even the young, may not run after money, but we do move in that direction at least at a fast trot. We may be Amish, but we're still Americans. Every one of us has taxes coming due, and we make do as best we can.

When it comes to choosing an occupation for a young

fellow, it's a simple affair. You're going to be what your dad is. Every Amishman might be a farmer at heart, but only one in three has the land to do it. Not to worry, though, for the Amish tend to spend a lot of time thinking this one out.

I had it pretty easy, being an only son. My dad was a builder, and so am I. Junior, that string bean of a fellow up the road, didn't have it so simple. He was a farmer, so the first two boys learned that. More children were coming along, so Junior retired from farming and laid concrete block. After he taught that to two more sons, he retired to making wooden pallets. Now that three of the boys are into that, I've heard some say he's about to retire again and start a sawmill. One thing is for sure: by the time he gets through the next five boys, Junior will have retired enough to build, clothe, and feed his own subdivision.

Things are a little simpler for the girls of a family because they are going to be what their mothers are—housewives. That has been, is, and always will be, the predominant Amish occupation for women. There have always been more housewives than anything else. The girls will put the skills they learned at their mother's apron to good use and make someone very happy someday. Before they do, though, there's nothing wrong with using those skills to make a dollar, even if it does involve a real collision of worlds.

One family south of us, down toward Cambridge, needed a maid. They're English, but that has nothing to do with Great Britain. *Englisch* is an Amish term for all others; you're either Amish or English. They put an ad in the paper, and the next day, here came Mary.

Mary was a good Amish girl. Her brown eyes had a permanent twinkle in them, and her poppa thought it a good idea that she work a while, earning a little money of her own. So the James family and Mary struck a deal, and she had a job.

In no time flat, Mary had that house spotless. She was such a good worker that she could even mind the small children too, being a nanny as well as a maid. Mary was such a good worker that it took the James family six weeks to realize there was a little quirk to Mary.

About once a week or so, Mary's back would hurt her. It hurt her so bad that she couldn't scrub the floors that day, but she could set the ironing board up in the living room and watch the children, too. With Mary being such a good worker, the family had no problem with the request.

It was six scorched shirts later before Fred and his wife discovered what was going on. The rules of Mary's congregation, called the *Ordnung,* were clear that she could not own a television. In fact, she was not permitted even to turn one on, but if somebody else did, there was nothing to keep her from watching it. Somehow she had mentioned that if the children would want the television on, that was fine. Mary became so engrossed that she then burned right through Fred's shirts.

Other arrangements have now been made. Mary comes to work an hour earlier each day. She works hard, harder than ever. In fact, she works so hard that she earns an hour's rest every afternoon. Right at the time something called "General Hospital" comes on.

Those lures of the city are easy to understand. I recall many years ago, when I was just five, going into town with my dad. Those were earlier times, and we didn't have indoor plumbing, nor had I seen it before. You can imagine the fascination for a young man to pull a lever and make water come rushing down. Naturally, I pulled it again, and again, and again, until I was dragged out of the rest room twenty minutes later by Dad.

For whatever reason, I didn't go back into that particular store for twenty-three years. Then I happened to saunter in, and the old man who had run it so many years ago was still there.

"Hey," he said as I walked in, "you come to buy something, or do you want to play with the toilets again?"

A man can never escape his past.

The teenage years in the Amish community must be the most wondrous time of life. Not only are the laboring skills growing, but so is something else called romance. In this time of great awakening, one thing is for sure. Once true love starts to bloom, we sure do get things backwards down the Peoli Road.

5

Romancing

Ever since time began for the Amish, around 1693, it's been a tradition that the unmarried young people gather together every other Sunday night and hold what's called a *singing*. The pattern is to join together in the barn or house where church had been that morning, boys on one side and girls on the other, and to sing good, pious church hymns. Afterward they have a little refreshment, everybody goes home, and that's it—in theory at least.

More than forty years ago a fellow slipped into a barn in Pennsylvania where there was a singing. He managed to get a picture, and, sure enough, theory and practice were somewhat different.

According to this photo, several of the young fellows were enjoying cold beer. A few of the girls were savoring cigarettes. Most importantly, there in the center of the barn floor was a radio, and several couples were in the process of dancing the jitterbug.

This always bothered me, more for always missing such wild times than for anything else. It tantalized me so much that I asked a neighbor, Freeman, if his wife ever danced the jitterbug at a singing. They're both from a congregation north of here, and I was thinking that they might know something I don't. After all, Freeman and his wife even went to Niagara Falls for a vacation once.

"Nope," he said, stroking his beard, "she didn't. But she could dance the pony and the stroll with the best of them."

What I always found amazing about our Peoli Road singings was the loss of memory which they inspired. I cannot recall a single singing when at least one young lady did not find herself absolutely helpless. How peculiar it was that the young lady had hitched up her buggy, driven to the singing, unhitched, gone in, and had a good time, only to magically forget how that horse gets hitched again when she's leaving. How strange that she was always really particular about who helped, too.

At any rate, romance begins and instantly steps behind a veil of secrecy. There's Amish all over Ohio, and I can't speak for any except down home. I can tell you that the Central Intelligence Agency would be proud of all the precautions taken just to make sure your business *stays* yours.

Let's say it's the next Saturday evening after a singing. At six o'clock the family gathers at the table for supper. In walks the young man of the house, in his Sunday clothes, and makes like there's nothing out of the ordinary. Sometime during the meal he mentions that he's figuring on going to town on business.

Nothing is said about this, even though every place of business closed an hour before. At least the old folks now know why the young fellow spent the entire afternoon alternating between washing the buggy and combing his hair. They also know that in another house nearby is a young lady, also in her Sunday clothes, making the announcement that she'll be taking a walk this evening.

Sure enough, just before dark, she is standing at a crossroads out of sight from both houses. That young man just happens by, and oh, my, yes, she would like a ride. As she climbs into the buggy, the flower of romance begins to bud.

Now, for the most part, these romances are tame affairs. An evening's ride, with maybe some ice-cream or snack at a local restaurant. Nothing at all like city romances, where the young fellow comes to her house and ends up being the prize bull on exhibition. No, the Amish parents don't know who their offspring is out with, but they do trust them. After all, they are Amish.

Just being Amish isn't a guarantee of sainthood, though, especially when it comes to romantic endeavors. Living so close to the English world—if not in philosophy then at least in physical proximity—does tend to cause the young people to interact from time to time. After all, Amish girls are some of the most beautiful and the fellows some of the most handsome young people on earth, at least in their own opinion. Thus it is inevitable that romance is just like crabgrass: it spreads across all boundaries anymore.

I distinctly recall the third Saturday of last October in that respect. Just after noon I had gone down to town on a little business. It was a pleasant day, fall cool and the like, as I tied up the hack by the courthouse. I had just knotted the rope when I happened to spy Emma standing across the square in the doorway to one of the stores.

Emma is Andy's youngest, the quiet one who does most

of her talking with her dark brown eyes. Maybe it was just a hunch, but even from a distance I had the impression that Emma preferred that I not see her. Her black bonnet had been replaced by a scarf, her jacket had a bit more fashion to it than what we see at church, and I'd say the hem of that oh-so-Amish dress had been temporarily turned up an inch or two.

She looked really nice, being polite to anyone who strolled past and happened to nod to her, but I'm not going to say I approve of such carrying on. I'm just glad we don't have it as bad as some. It seems that the closer our people get to the big city, the more we notice the dual personality tending to appear.

The fellow who comes our way selling power tools was the one who first tipped me off to this. He's from the Wooster area, and one Friday evening, he decided to take his wife to some big hotel thereabouts for dinner. From what he said, they'd just finished and were paying the bill when he saw four or five Amish girls going into the ladies' room.

Since Paul does so much business with the Amish, he figured he'd wait and see if he knew some old friends. When the door opened again and the young ladies reappeared, he figured that even if he did know them, he had better not admit it right then. Leather skirts, silk blouses, and no sign of a prayer cap anywhere told him it was the girls' night out.

Since I didn't want to be in that situation, I stuck close to the side of the buildings as I strolled about my business. Fortunately for my curiosity, in just a minute a young fellow pulled up to the curb in his automobile. By the smile on her face, Emma had an afternoon planned. As she started to get into the car, her jacket parted to reveal she was wearing a most unusual sweatshirt over her dress. All of a sudden everything fell into place.

A fall Saturday means college football here in Ohio. Emma was wearing an Ohio State shirt, and it was the day of the big homecoming game. Her next four hours were well taken care of. Her brothers would be waiting for Monday's paper for an account of the game while she, the sly one, would play ignorant and have seen it all. If that's what they call woman's lib, I think I'm all for it.

When Suzanna came to Holmes County on a college-based tour of the area, she also found herself in one of these interfaith relationships, receiving the attention of a young Amishman. Although she appeared quite normal and seemed to be the average college girl, this group quickly discovered that she had a problem. When they finally got the problem solved, I'd say all parties found what a small world it really is.

Suzanna had been living at home in Germany only five weeks before this vanload of scholars went to Holmes County. She had just arrived in the United States as a foreign exchange student. Her sponsors, knowing she had written a school paper on the peculiar Americans called Amish, had signed her up for the trip.

That was all well and good, in theory at least, but then the little problem set in. Suzanna could read and write English very well. She could speak it, too, but not like Americans do and certainly not as fast as city people do. Twenty miles outside of Columbus, the poor girl was confused.

They all worried about Suzanna, trying their best to have her keep pace until the second stop of the day. They had just pulled into Mount Hope when one of the ladies on the trip came up with a plan. Suzanna spoke German, and the Amish speak a dialect of the same. That vanload took a vote and decided Suzanna was going to find an Amish to talk to. If she didn't, they weren't going to let her back in the van.

Half believing this dire threat, Suzanna set off for the local hardware. This being her lucky day, there was an Amish lady doing some shopping in there. The young lady summoned all her courage and struck up a conversation.

I can't speak for the rest of the world, but being Amish, the next best thing to discovering a relative is to find somebody from the old country. Even though the roots of the faith are in Switzerland, that's close enough. This Amish lady was so pleased to meet Suzanna that she almost talked her ear off.

Somewhere in the midst of this conversation, the door to the store opened and in strolled the Amish lady's oldest son. He was Plain, but he had an eye for a good looking girl. In just a moment, he was in this conversation as well.

Somehow time slipped away in there that day. Suddenly they realized that it was time for Suzanna to rejoin her group and go on. I dare say there was some sadness in parting until the young fellow did a little quick thinking. He ambled over to the counter, got a piece of paper and a pencil, and did some quick sketching.

"Now," he said, finishing off his map, "if . . . no, when you come back, this is how to find our farm. We would like you to come and visit. If you do, I would like to give you a ride in my buggy."

With Momma Amish grinning the way she was, Suzanna had no choice but to agree. Let us close the glimpse into this friendship by saying that Suzanna did come to visit, the young fellow did get a chance to show off his rig, and. . . . Well, we'll just worry about that later.

Romance progresses by degree down the Peoli Road. It won't be long before you can count on a young couple to do their share of lap-sitting, but we even do that backwards. Yep, he sits on her lap going down the road. Come now, somebody has to drive.

Where they're all headed is for one very special night. We do things old-fashioned back home. I can't tell you if any other congregation is still like us, but it doesn't matter. What does matter is that a young couple has their lives in order with each other and their church. Everything is set as he lets her out of the buggy that evening. Nothing's said, but somehow it's been sensed.

The young lady will go to her room, but not to sleep. She's too busy listening for the sound of his buggy coming up the lane. It's the first time he's done this, and when she hears those wheels, she starts intently watching her bedroom ceiling for the beam of his flashlight.

It could be that if you'd do such a stunt in the city, you'd be arrested. Down the Peoli Road, he's just said, "Will you marry me?"

When she comes downstairs, opens the door, and they stay up all night making plans to meet her parents, the answer is "Yes!"

Maybe it was just a hunch, but I was awake one night when Sis slipped in. It was just a few minutes later that I heard the wheels. I slipped over to the window, spied out, and from the buggy jumped Junior Weaver.

Junior took out his light, got it all set, aimed it, pushed the button, and nothing happened. He shook it, jiggled it, pushed the button, and nothing. He hit it on the side of the buggy, pushed the button, but there was nothing. The dog started barking, and all of a sudden, the front door opened, and there was Dad.

Real slowlike, Dad shut the door from the inside, and Junior got in a rush. He was shaking the light, hitting the buggy, and spitting on the flashlight. The dog was barking, the rooster was crowing, and the front door opened again. Real slowlike, Dad walked across the porch, down the steps, and over to Junior. Pop reached in his pocket and pulled out two flashlight batteries.

"Here," Dad said, handing Junior the batteries. "I suppose she could have done worse."

I had my own problems a few years back when it came to romance. There was a beautiful girl living in a neighboring congregation, and I just thought she was swell. It didn't bother me that some say she had come our way with a purpose. She was from well northwest of here, up where there are fewer eligible men than around these parts.

It could be that Mary was making her move before she got invited to any more of what the Amish called "older single girls" outings. You might call it a spinsters' club, but that's neither here nor there. All that does matter is that I did have an eye for her.

The romance started off nice and slow, like it should. It did progress by degree and was going quite well by my estimation. It was even going so well that I gave thought to marrying the poor girl. Then, suddenly, she sent word through a mutual friend that she didn't care to see me again. She had discovered I'd told her a lie.

I felt bad about this, for lying is a sin. I felt worse, for she was a fine Christian woman, and I didn't want to hurt her. To be honest, there is yet another reason that really makes me feel bad. I don't know which lie she caught me at. There were so many.

Just as this dark moment passed in my life, a spot of brightness appeared. It was the last warm day of fall last year when I just happened by Mill Pond. Now we're not much for the bathing suits, being sort of expensive for all you get, and, yep, there was Marvin's oldest girl taking a swim.

Amanda is twenty-two and hasn't married, but not because of her looks, not with those blue eyes and that chestnut hair. She stands up for herself, and that scares the fellows. When I saw I had a chance to have a little fun with her, I slipped down there real quiet, snatched up her clothes, and made a run for it.

She saw what was happening, jumped out of the water, kept one of those big cement tubs in front of her, and shouted, "Hey!"

I stopped and turned around.

"I'd say you think you're smart, Eli," she said.

"Could be," I said back, "but I'd say you think there's a bottom in that tub."

Yep, we're all backwards down home, doing so much like this romancing the old-fashioned way. You never see Amish couples hanging all over each other or the like, but enough love is there for two to share. Since you don't find Amish people at that divorce court and families do tend to be large, it almost makes you think we're doing something right all along.

6

Rumschpringe

In the rotation of crops there was a recognized season for wild oats; but they were not sown more than once.
—Edith Wharton

There is no greater loan than a sympathetic ear.
—Frank Tyger

There is more than romance afoot for the teenager in the Amish community. Besides finding a prospective mate, the young are expected to experience what is known as *Rumschpringe,* the running-around years. That is when you try to see what life is like on the outside, with the knowledge that nine times out of ten you'll come back where you belong.

A 90 percent success ratio is nothing to sneeze at, I suppose. That's the way it is in Ohio, though. For every ten children, just one will find his way into the electrified world. Even the ones who are staying, as I mentioned with those Wooster girls, aren't above tasting what's just beyond the next hill. Sometimes, though, we're just not prepared for what all we get into.

We admit that some do their share of drinking. Others carry on like wild heathens. Buggymaker John even moved to New York City, and I know he must have seen it all, even if he didn't do it all. Some even go so far as to buy an automobile, hiding it at a neighbor's place or the local gas station.

One fellow did just that: he bought a car and kept it down the way at a service station. How he could impress the guys and the girls, too, with that two-toned 1968 Buick Special with air conditioning and automatic transmission! The one he especially wanted to impress was the little dark-haired beauty named Rachel, who was about as wild as he was.

Somehow this fellow and Rachel ended up sitting in that car one afternoon on the hilltop overlooking the Peoli Valley. With talking and such, they were occupied until just before dark. They'd had the gravel lane to themselves all that time until they saw a buggy coming slowly up the hill behind them.

The buggy pulled right up beside them and stopped. Very slowly the canvas side curtain was raised and the stately white beard of Ammon Swartzentruber appeared. It was a tense moment, for not only was he a pillar of the church, Ammon was also Rachel's uncle.

The old man waited until the car driver nodded in greeting, and then he said, "Do you mind receiving a piece of advice, boy?"

The young fellow shook his head, bracing himself for a stern lecture at the best.

"When you kiss her, keep your foot off the brake pedal. My wife and I were sitting down below thinking you were flashing some sort of Morse code at us."

With that, he dropped the curtain, made a U-turn with the buggy, and headed for home. The only way this story can end is to tell you that I had that car sold the next Monday.

This is a growing community hereabouts, and not just from young folk marrying and starting families. Maybe every other year we'll get immigrants, Amish from other areas of Ohio looking for cheaper land or a little more space. With each new family comes new ideas, doing some things the way they did it back in Wayne County or wherever. I have heard that some newcomer boys use those cars they've got so carefully hidden to go as far as that amusement place, Cedar Point.

Some may be critical, but I'm not among them. It's not that I'd care to see that place, but I do have a pretty good memory of my own *Rumschpringe*. In those days, we did our adventuring in the hidden car to a place called Chippewa Lake Amusement Park, over toward Medina, Ohio.

It just happened that some of us were up that way a short time back, going to the auction at Creston. As the sale wasn't that much and we had some time, we decided to go the last ten miles and see what the scene of so many good times looked like these days.

You can imagine my surprise as we rounded the last bend to discover the park still there, but not open anymore. The buildings seemed to be standing, and the shells for most of the rides, but it was all overgrown. I can't recall the last time we were there. Looking at how rundown it was, those days seemed centuries ago.

We went up to the gate, all padlocked shut, to get a closer look. I think every one of us in the van had some memory of the place. Ivan was talking of the fun house; Leroy was raving about that speedboat they used to run on the lake. My longing was for that roller coaster. It scared me to

death, and I couldn't wait to get back on it. Looking at the park again was really strange. It just seemed that somebody walked away one night and said good-bye forever.

As we were gawking through the fence, a car pulled up, and a young lady got out. We were thinking at first that she might tell us to be moving on, but far from it. She lived right close by the park, in one of those cottages by the lake. She was so wild about the place that she even wrote a book about it.

From what she said, even before the Civil War, folks used to come there to picnic and have a good time. As she was talking about those good times and famous people who came there, I began thinking back a few years. It was fun to go there, good clean fun. There was no drinking or carrying on there, unlike some other places. It was a family place, people didn't need to spend a lot of money, and they had a good feeling when they left each night.

As I looked at how deserted the park was, instead of giving me a good feeling, it was making me feel empty that day. It was as though an old friend had slipped away. Ivan asked the lady if she thought the place would ever open up again. My spirits rose a bit when she said it was possible. Somebody always seemed to be interested lately, and that grand old lady of amusement parks just might get it going. She sure was trying hard enough.

Right about then the biggest flock of Canadian geese I'd ever seen came flying right over us. You could hardly hear for the honking as they settled in the Chippewa Lake. That's about the most beautiful music in the world to me, but this time it caused my mind to play tricks on me.

I could almost hear the wheels of the roller-coaster cars again. A band was playing up in that magnificent ballroom. There was laughter, even if it was only in my mind, coming from people having a good time. A good time. That was a good memory to hang onto. Seeing a place like that come back to life is a hope worth holding onto as well.

My wallet was out, and without a second thought, I said, "I'll take one of your books if you've got one." I was well pleased to buy one. Just last night I was thumbing through my copy again to relive a most pleasant time. Maybe it wasn't wild enough for some of these computer-addicted ones today, but it was all the enjoyment I could handle.

With all the mischief some can find these days, I wish that lady well in getting a decent place back on the map. I don't know if she is well acquainted with the Amish people. Maybe it was just words to her when we said that when she got those padlocks off, we'd be back. That wasn't a promise, lady. That's fact.

Rumschpringe seems to vary by degree among the Amish. Owning a car and hiding it might be rather wild here, but absolutely silly nearer to Berlin. Some of their unbaptized young not only buy the car, they even drive it home. It all depends on how far you care to carry it, I suppose.

Wild Raymond carried it about as far as any human would care to, judging by the story I heard. I don't know what all he did in his *Rumspchringe,* nor do I want to. All I know the fact that he was out joyriding in a car with some English girls one night. They were going down Old 21 too fast.

The car went off the road. One girl was killed, and Raymond—well, we didn't know his outcome for a long time. He was in the hospital for three months, then bedridden at home for six more months. The steady stream of visitors he'd had in the hospital became a flood at home. Everybody wished him good cheer and such, but one visitor really bothered the family.

This fellow came only once. He's the kind who was always clowning around and telling jokes. But he didn't have much to say when he came to see Raymond. He just sat like he was thinking about his own wild days. How close he'd come to such a disaster! It didn't make sense to the family, this change in character, but it doesn't matter. I only hope Raymond's family never finds out how much I love them and that I never forget the risks I ran.

7

Together

Shunning works a little bit like an electric fence around a pasture.
—former Amishman

The nice thing about teamwork is that you always have others on your side.
—Margaret Carty

It was three weeks ago last Sunday that Raymond was baptized into the congregation. He has, like so many before, made a vow to follow the rules of the congregation for life, that *Ordnung* I mentioned. It is his most serious decision, for he knows it is far better never to make his vow than to make it and later break it. To break his vow with the congregation leaves no choice other than to be shunned.

Some say there are twelve different kinds of horse-and-buggy Amish in Ohio today. Nowhere is the shunning as serious as down the Peoli Road. Here we have no dealings with one who has fallen away: neither in buying nor selling, eating nor drinking, speaking nor listening to such a person (1 Corinthians 5:11). It's brutal and a fact of life, but it always struck me as strange that it didn't seem to bother Mose when the Amish church ran his boy out.

Run him out we did, because he thought for himself. He read and he wondered, questioning everything. Such behavior didn't sit well, and it didn't sit at all when he went out and started courting an English girl.

They gave him three chances to bring her into our fold, but he wouldn't have it (Matthew 18:15-18). It was her world he wanted to share forever, not his. Jonas knew the shunning was coming, so he didn't even show up at church that Sunday. He'd already said his good-byes to his friends and was long gone.

Maybe I just didn't give it too much thought until last February. We were all in Columbus at the big draft horse auction when I noticed Mose wasn't too interested in the horses. He kept checking the time until about noon, when he eased away from the crowd.

For whatever reason, I followed at a distance. Mose wandered around a bit and then made a beeline to a pay phone. I watched him fish out a quarter, tap out a well-known number, and for the next half hour had quite a conversation.

I don't know what was said. I wouldn't tell you if I did, for as he hung up and turned around, Mose had a grin that has been reserved for grandpas since time began. For a little while longer, the world was just fine to him. Sure, his boy was run out for wanting another kind of life, but he's still blood. We might have run him out of the valley, but not from Moses' heart.

A few years before I came into this world, another fellow was excommunicated from a Wayne County congregation. Instead of accepting his church's decision, this fellow took his affairs to a court of law. He sued his bishop and

preachers, demanding that they not only stop the shunning but pay him damages as well.

Not being much for the legal system, the Amish holy men didn't put up much of a defense. Their argument was that our faith was one of tradition, that we are bound together by holding to basic principles. Our people find contentment in security. Coupled with our tradition goes the confidence that our neighbors think as we do. Through our support of each other and faith in the Lord, we will survive even as pilgrims in a strange land.

Unfortunately, the legal system put more stock in the rights of the individual over the good of the community. The convenience of one individual couldn't be sacrificed even if it threatened the good of the congregation in holding to its conviction. The judge awarded damages and ordered the congregation to stop shunning. In fact, he declared the act of the shunning illegal.

Well, the fellow got the money he wanted, and I really do hope he enjoyed every penny of it. Funny thing, though, he stayed shunned, and all Amish continue to shun to this day. For a while longer we'll keep supporting the Constitution of the United States. We won't tell Uncle Sam how to run his business, and he won't tell us what language to pray in.

Perhaps more than in any other church, the rite of baptism is a passage into adulthood for the Amish. Baptism is more than the outward signs of a woman changing her style of cape and shawl and a man growing his beard. It is an acceptance of, and by, a fellowship of believers and a true beginning into a lifetime of heavenly service.

Back in 1525, when a group called the Swiss Brethren was formed, infant baptism was the norm. Those Brethren, our forefathers of the Plain church, didn't go for that. They figured that only an adult could make the choice to follow Christ, and so do we.

We figure if a young man and woman have a career lined up, have a good idea who the spouse will be, and have survived *Rumschpringe,* they're ready for life. Generally that's between the ages of eighteen and twenty-four. That's the way it's been done for a long time, and like just about everything else, that's the way it will stay.

Being accepted into full fellowship of a congregation is like a license. You can now marry in the church when you're ready. More importantly, you're an equal to all other members. You respect the elderly and the officials of the church, certainly, but you are also expected to carry your end. In the Amish world, that end is defined as work.

It's been a good year, a great year, for the farmers around here. Enough rain and such as that. As much as I enjoy pounding nails as a carpenter, I'll take the chance to help out in harvest any time. It was fun working with the threshing crews in late July. It's even better taking a week's vacation to harvest the corn this year. One hundred forty-four stalks to the shock. As great as that is, though, it was nothing compared to when Junior Miller needed a barn.

Two summers ago, heavy storms went through the country and brought a lot of rain and even more lightning. Sure enough, one of those bolts hit Junior's barn. In what seemed like a minute, the whole place was in flames. They did manage to save the dairy herd, but the only other thing left was a big pile of ash.

A couple of days later, Jacob came down to Junior's. Jake is what's known as a boss carpenter, a master barn builder. He sat, just sat, for an eight-hour day and did nothing but look at the rubble. He didn't make any notes or sketches, nothing, but when he got up at five that evening, he was ready to build a barn.

Word went out that Jake was ready. Through word of mouth, letters, an ad in a newspaper for the Amish called *The Budget,* and in churches, it was announced that there'd be a barn raising in two weeks on a Saturday.

On the Thursday of raising week, a mason crew came in

and laid the foundation. On Saturday morning, as the sun started up, the buggies started rolling in. Soon cars and vanloads came along from further distances. At seven that morning, six hundred men set to work.

Jake was the boss. If he told you the beam was to be sixteen feet, then that's what it was. If he wanted you in the rafters, then that's where you worked. He was just like a ringmaster, directing a building project with the blueprint etched in his mind. It didn't matter if you were a farmer who had never hammered a thing or a master carpenter that day. You did what Jake told you, knowing he was right.

At noontime, it was the women's turn to take charge. They spread a feast like you can't imagine. So much and so good it was like watching a magic show. Something was put on the table, and it just disappeared.

By five that afternoon, the last buggy headed for home. Where the ashes had been was now home to a barn 180 feet wide, 250 long, and four stories high. Not only built, but roofed and whitewashed as well.

There is no plaque marking the occasion, no sign of self-congratulations at the barn today. Junior did express his thanks in church and in the newspaper, but it wasn't necessary. It's just a part of being Amish. Like a team of finely matched draft horses, the Plain People put aside their differences and pull together to help. There were a lot of tired muscles, but we can hardly wait to do it again.

8

Business and Bureaucrats

A dinner lubricates business.
—James Boswell

*Hospitality is making your guests feel at home, even
though you wish they were.*
—Unknown

Before you go to thinking that everything the Amish
touch turns to gold, perhaps I should mention something.
Those of the world sometimes get a real bargain in dealing
with the Amish. Sometimes they get more than they bar-
gained for, too.

Mr. Jones was getting along in years when he knew he
needed another corncrib. He couldn't build it, but since he
was living on the northern edge of an Amish community,
he figured he could find a carpenter or two. He put an ad
in the local paper, and the next day brought two young
Amish carpenters to his door.

Yes, they could build the corncrib, and the price was
right. There were a few conditions, though. They could
build the crib in two days if they could stay overnight.
They couldn't stay overnight unless they brought their
families.

Jones is no fool. He knew Ohio's Amish average seven children to a family, so he checked. With only six little ones between them, there was no problem. Ignoring his sixth sense, Mr. Jones struck the deal.

The next morning, near ten o'clock, the Amish families arrived and set to work. Work they did, hard work, right up to suppertime. Yes, they would be delighted to share supper with the Jones family. One Amish wife thanked Mrs. Jones profusely and told her not to worry about breakfast. They had brought some "things" for that. The carpenters put away their tools, got cleaned up, and the adventure began.

The Amish sat down at the table, said their silent grace, and proceeded to eat everything not nailed down. Not one slice of bread but six or seven. One fellow liked the cooking so much that he ate a whole chicken. They weren't done until the table was bare.

Everyone retired to the living room, and the Plain ones were gracious guests. They made pleasant conversation, in between belches, and had a nice visit until eight o'clock. That was bedtime. They appreciated the Jones' gesture of separate bedrooms, but it wasn't necessary. After all, they were family, and off they went.

Somehow the room that was selected was that of the Jones family's oldest daughter, the one away at college. The room that had the stereo, which just happened to get turned on. Turned on to WMMS, rock and roll in Cleveland, with the volume up to eight notches out of ten, and that's where it stayed.

Well into evening, in between songs on the radio, Mr. Jones heard a "bonk," then another "bonk" coming from the room with the Amish. He tiptoed over and carefully opened the door to survey a most amazing scene.

The adults were stretched out on the floor, all snoring as loud as the radio. The children had found football helmets and baseball bats. The "bonk" was a bat connecting to a helmet. Mr. Jones put his finger to his lips and then made a sign to kill the radio. Without the radio blaring and with the snoring now reverberating through the walls, he stumbled back to his own room.

You probably know how well the smell of bacon frying can carry. You can imagine that smell at five-thirty in the morning. That's the time the Amish ladies were up. At six-thirty, hammers were being swung outside. With no more chance of rest, Mr. and Mrs. Jones staggered out to watch the project come to completion.

By ten that morning, a new corncrib was finished. The Amish loaded up, took their pay, and with smiles and handshakes all around were off. The Jones couple watched from the porch as the buggies went out the lane. With one final wave, the Amish turned onto the main road and were gone.

As the buggies disappeared into the distance, Mr. Jones turned to his wife and said, "You know, they did do a nice job. The price was great. I was thinking, next year I may be needing a barn. . . ."

History records that Mrs. Jones didn't talk to him for three weeks.

I got wind of this saga the last time I stopped by to get some harness repaired up the road. As meaningful as discussions can be down at the mill, when it comes to exchanging vital information, there's no place hereabouts that can compare to Peoli Harness. From what I can tell, Little Stutzman's place is roughly equivalent to the English barbershop. It's the place for true insight, complete with commentary, on the rest of the world. Take, for example, the puzzle of why Japanese shoes are so cheap.

"I can tell you why," Stutzman was saying that first day I was in to get some work harness made. "It's them boats. Those Japanese people send over great big boats to the San Francisco dock. There's a guy standing there, probably from Texas or Wyoming, who has a whole bunch of leather hides for sale.

"When those Japanese see all this good leather, they buy it all up and load it into their boat. Then they turn the boat around and head to Tokyo. The whole time they're floating across the Pacific, there's hundreds of Japanese people, all down in the hold, cutting up those hides and forming shoes.

"They're not near done when they get back to Tokyo, but that doesn't matter. They've got enough finished that they can load all sorts of cardboard in the hold, too. They check their mail and then head right back toward San Francisco.

"About halfway across, all the shoes have been made. Those people put away their shoe tools and start folding cardboard into boxes. They've got it timed so well that they're slapping on the last label just as the boat's tying up to the dock. Then they start it all over again.

"That's why Japanese shoes are so cheap. You can't get people to work like that in this country."

I didn't want to burst Little Stutzman's bubble, but I don't think the Japanese work like that, either. There's no sense in arguing, though. That's what he's heard and now repeated a thousand times. Around Peoli Harness, that's all it takes to constitute fact. I'm just glad Stutzman makes harness and doesn't write for the newspaper. Although, given some things I've read, maybe he does.

The Amish have no problem with working hard. It's hoped that if you die in the cause of laboring, it might give you a leg up on salvation. Nothing for certain, for that is vain, and we do strive to avoid vanity, but it might help. Hard work sets a good example for the young and old alike and even for the outsider.

Some time ago, long before me, an Amish family took in a foster boy. Once in a while the Plain People do that, not to add another member to the faith, but because children need a good home. A good home is just what this family gave Jack. They cared for him and taught him to love his work. So they had more than a little regret when Jack turned eighteen and went off to make his own way.

It wasn't long before Jack settled down in Indiana and had a family of his own. Jack always fondly recalled his Berlin family, even as things turned bad at home. Bad they were, for Jack's boy, John, was a real troublemaker.

John never could stay out of trouble. He stole something as a boy and got sent to the Navy. Then he deserted that and raised all sorts of heartache, not only in Indiana, but in Illinois and Ohio, too. One time he had a real fracas in Lima. For all the problems he caused, John never once came to Berlin, even though some of his associates had their own problems not far from Berlin.

Some say that it was because there's nothing in Berlin that John never came that way. Could be, though, that John always remembered what his father had said about the Amish. How he respected them, and how they treated him with respect, too. The more I mull it over, it just could be that the line that marks Amish country was always considered unpassable by Jack's boy, John Dillinger.

Yet sometimes the law comes looking for the Amish. Oh, yes, we've got ourselves a desperate criminal type right here in our community, at least according to some. That rascal Leroy, the one with the sawmill, is our equivalent of a Dillinger, being so ruthless that he burns scraps of oak lumber in his yard.

That's right! Burning sweet-smelling excess from his woodshop in an orderly pile is such a crime that our environmental protection people threatened Leroy with a $25,000 fine and a year in jail if he didn't stop, and stop right now! It didn't matter that folks have been burning wood along this road for almost two hundred years. It didn't matter that the rendering plant, the one right by Peoli Ridge School, puts out plenty of stink and now wants to burn rubber tires, too. No, sir, it was Leroy who was the criminal, and he had to be stopped.

To say this caused some worry with Leroy, as well as the rest of us, is one of the year's biggest understatements. Being simple people, we know our words can't be heard when we try to speak over the shouting of lawyers or government types. It seemed like these enforcement people were just looking for an easy case to help their statistics, which doesn't seem too fair. There didn't appear to be much we could do about this mess.

Just about the time we were all feeling low about this, a stranger came calling in our valley. Mike was his name, a young fellow who asked some questions and listened even more. We thought he might be from the government at first and were standoffish. When we found out he was a newspaper reporter, that was a little better, but still a lot of lips remained buttoned shut. We're a private people for the most part, and more than one wondered what this Mike was up to.

He visited there at Leroy's and got some of the facts. Some say they later saw him looking at that stink plant. Others saw him watching Amos turning the soil with that magnificent team of Belgians he has. One or two even say Mike was seen watching school let out children who were miniature versions of their parents. He saw them heading for home right past the rendering plant we call pollution but the government calls business.

About two weeks later, Leroy's got a copy of some big city newspaper in the mail. They thought it strange, since they weren't subscribers and had never heard of it before. The parents almost threw it away when Junior, the youngest one, spotted something about an Amishman and the government.

Sure enough, Mike the reporter had gotten the story into print. I saw the paper, and my opinion is that those bureaucrats didn't end up looking too good. More like fools, come to think of it. Maybe that's why it wasn't too long before they made a quick peace with Leroy and haven't been seen around these parts since.

As for Mike, we haven't seen him around here either. He's more than welcome, but maybe it's just that he's a bit standoffish. Like so many others, he could be thinking that the Amish world is bound to family, and outsiders need not apply. Yet we want him to know that sometimes things around here are a matter of the heart more than blood. In case Mike ever realizes that, we'll keep a slice of pie handy.

9

Auctions and Talk

To amuse you with stories. . . .
—Edmund Burke

*One way to prevent conversation from being boring is to
say the wrong thing.*
—Frank Sheed

What dumbfounds me personally is how some people
never seem to be able to find anything to do. They sit, doing what some call vegetating, and end up having nothing
to show for it. Somehow those with time to waste try to
spend it with those who don't. I'm not saying Amish people
don't have idle time. Work takes a good share of the day,
but we can always make space for some fun. And we don't
need any television or computer for a good time either.

I can't think of a single Amish family that doesn't spend
some time every evening reading the Bible. We like
Luther's translation, High German in a Gothic script. If
that isn't enough to inspire one, then there's always a book
called *Martyrs Mirror*. That volume records the persecu-
tions of earlier days, when being different meant hard
times.

The Amish do have to save some reading energies for

that weekly newspaper I mentioned, *The Budget.* That grand paper comes out once a week from Sugarcreek, Ohio. It is so good that the paper has inspired a recycling movement down at the mill.

Jake and Andy, brothers-in-law that have been here since time began, run the mill, and they have a company subscription for the paper. All the loafers know what time the mail comes, so we all mosey down after that on Thursday afternoons. It's a real ritual these days, making sure the paper gets read.

Jake will get the mail, open up the paper, and read all the big block ads. Then he folds it up and puts it in the trash. Andy will go over, pull the paper out of the can, and study the classifieds. When he's all done, he folds it up and puts it back in the can.

About the time the paper hits the bottom of the trash bin, Ammon is up off the bench and headed for it. He'll pull out the first section, the one with the auction announcements, and read those. Back in the trash it goes so Junior can get up and pull out the section that has news from Pennsylvania congregations. It's such a great newspaper that on and on this goes until we all get to read our favorite part. Then on Friday we can tell each other what we've read.

If it seems foolish to you that grown men would go through such a ritual, you're not alone. The thought did cross my mind, too, but it only took once to learn.

It was the first Thursday I had been among the trustees. I saw Jake look through the paper and put it in the can. Natural as could be, I said, "Hey, why don't you pass that over here?"

Natural as could be, Jake shot right back, "Why don't

you spend fifty cents and buy your own paper?"

Given a choice between spending fifty cents and trash picking, I'll keep recycling, if you don't mind.

We used to subscribe to a city paper at our house, but finally decided it just wasn't worth the money we were spending. Don't get me wrong; it was a good paper and all, but it just seemed to be filled with a lot of things we weren't interested in. If it wasn't the advertising for a bunch of stuff we've got no use for, then it was what some call "news" that caused us to lose interest quickly.

There's a lot of bad in the world, but we knew that before the newspaper filled in the gory details. We don't see many foreign people along Peoli way, so we hardly find ourselves concerned with their affairs. As I recall, about the only concerns I've had of late are the weather and whether or not we can make a little money on our next project. That worries me enough that I don't need to fret over things I can't change.

Some say it wasn't too long after the Amish broke away from the Mennonites in 1693, that the Plain People discovered something unique about the human body. They discovered what is now called a mouth and that they could speak words. It has progressed to the point today that whenever two or more Amish gather together, good talk breaks out.

The Amish love to visit. It's even more fun than reading. Visit family, visit friends, just visit and share the time. Maybe visiting is almost a lost art among the city crowd, but it's honed to perfection among the buggy crowd. If you really want some good talk, maybe you'd just better investigate what's known as a horse auction.

The second Saturday of every month finds the barn in Mt. Hope, up in Holmes County, packed with the fellows for the horse auction. Those are good sales, but we generally save our energies for the big sale of the year in Columbus. It comes the first Tuesday and Wednesday of February each year. How big? About seven hundred head of draft horses and five thousand people, most in the black felt hats or bonnets. It's a real spectacle that was more spectacular than usual last year.

The sale had slowed down that Tuesday afternoon, so a few of us went out for a stroll. Some of us noticed a lot of city folk going into another building close by and thought we'd investigate. We wandered along the back of the building, jiggling doors, and sure enough, one was open. Since it was open, we just made our way into something called a vacation and travel show.

To say it was interesting would be an understatement, but it was no horse sale. We'd seen just about everything we cared to look at when up stepped a policeman.

He nodded and wondered if he could help us. We appreciated it, but it wasn't necessary. Then he wondered how we got in. When he heard that we had come in the unlocked back door, he figured that we ought to go back out that same way. That, or pay the $4.50 admission at the front gate. It should go without saying that out the door we went.

To this day my associates are mystified as to how that policeman was so clever. There were more than a thousand people in that travel show. The fellows don't understand how he knew we were the only ones who didn't pay.

I'm not going to say, but I think I've got a clue. Indeed, there were a thousand in the throng. Perhaps it had something to do with the fact that of the thousand, there were only six of us with black felt hats, beards but no mustaches, and button pants. Something to do with standing out in a crowd.

Women are not exempt from sale excitement, either, I might note. They may not care for the horses like I do, but put the quilts up on the block, and you'd better stand back. This I know firsthand.

We were going to have an auction to raise money for Peoli Ridge School. Some foolish character announced that they were going to start selling the handstitched quilts in fifteen minutes. It was my unfortunate luck to be standing along the line between the food tent and the sale ring. It only took two weeks for the bruises and trample marks to heal up.

A local auctioneer was running the sale. He's an older

fellow who's got a good chant and keeps the crowd loose. Bid quick, or he'll leave you in his wake, not wasting time bugging people to bid a quarter more. Most importantly, he's dealt with the Amish in auctions and in his business. It may sound strange, but that tends to prevent embarrassment sometimes.

One time back, some English friends took us down to a sale well southeast of us. The sale bill looked good, and I'd say we were excited about it. Once we got there and looked over the goods, we had our eye on several items that just might come in at a bargain price.

The problem came when I went to register to bid. Around here, you just tell them your name. A man's word goes a long way. Down at this sale, things tended to run a little different.

Real patientlike, I waited my turn to get a number. The young lady who was cashiering must not have been having a good day. She was sort of snippy, asking to see my driver's license.

I looked at her kind of stupid and told her I didn't have such as that. Then she wanted a credit card. I'll tell you, I go for those less than a driver's license. She seemed real ticked off and asked for my Social Security card. When I told her, being self-employed, I was exempt from that, she laid down the law.

"Well, you can't bid," she snapped. "Next."

I shrugged, dumbfounded that our great society no longer accepts greenbacks. Figuring that was it, I started to leave when I realized the fellow behind me had let out a string of words I don't care to use. "If you can't trust those guys, who can you trust?" was all I can repeat from him.

The cashier was insistent—no identification meant no

number. This fellow dressed in coveralls and old work boots gave her a look, didn't say any more, and marched right out the door. Since I didn't want to make trouble, I headed out that way myself. I'd no more gotten out the door when here came this fellow back, now with the auctioneer in tow.

That auctioneer took one look and told me to come along. Back inside we went, bucking to the head of the line. It was short and sweet, with the auctioneer saying, "Register him."

The young lady started to argue, but it was cut short. I don't recall the exact words, but it was something about cashiers being a dime a dozen. I felt bad, really bad, about the trouble, but the two fellows would have none of it.

"Forget it," the auctioneer said. "I need business from you guys."

The other fellow, once he got over his mad, cooled down and was real pleasant. I was so grateful for him standing up for me, a total stranger, that I gave him one of our business cards and told him I hoped to return the favor. He seemed grateful in return, giving me one of his cards.

I've got no reason to doubt what his card said, after seeing the way some people talked to this new friend. Funny though, if you're smart enough to cashier a sale, wouldn't you be smart enough to recognize your county commissioner, too?

There's one kind of sale that has priority over any horse or quilt auction. When a family or an individual has racked up hospital bills, that's an auction we don't miss.

You see, the Amish don't live by insurance. They live by the assurance of their community. Each family is frugal to offset those bills when they come, but sometimes that isn't enough. Sometimes you have to be reminded how much some folks care.

Ruth is a fine woman, a tower of strength in her congregation. It hurt everyone when she took sick. It hurt even more when it was found that she would need a liver transplant to survive.

The family made the arrangements, and she had the operation. After the operation, when they knew she'd be just fine, the hospital was kind enough to give them a bill for a quarter of a million dollars. The hospital people were good about it though; they didn't need to be paid for sixty days.

When word spread of such city generosity, the community took over. A charity auction was organized for one Saturday. With news spreading throughout Amish Ohio, the idea was to try to retire as much of that debt as possible. For many days, all Ruth and her family could do was wait.

That Saturday came, and the auctioneer started his chant at nine. Everything was donated, and all proceeds, even from the food concession, were going to Ruth. The people kept coming, they kept bidding, and they kept buying. The hammer fell for the last time at eight that evening. When the accounting was done, $335,000 was collected. It felt really good to be a human being that day.

As remarkable as this bit of charity is, this sale will always be remembered by the crowd hereabouts as my coming-out party. Thanks to a quirk of fate and some fast thinking, I was finally recognized for the talents I have developed over the years. In the blink of an eye, I was proclaimed Community Storyteller, source of an evening's entertainment, and imparter of wisdom. From my side of the fence, all I was doing was trying to stay alive.

Several of us had come up from Peoli to Ruth's sale, more to do visiting than anything else. We were standing off in the yard, talking and telling some jokes. We'd been clowning around for some time when an older fellow made his way over and joined in the community circle.

One thing led to another, and before long this fellow was a part of the conversation as well. He seemed quite interested to hear that we were from the Peoli area. He'd never been there but had heard some about it. It turned out that he had a daughter living and working not far from there.

He introduced himself as Jonas Miller. I was trying to fight a hunch and found myself asking if he was the Jonas from Millersburg or the one from the Sugarcreek area.

"Oh, Sugarcreek," he said. "Do you know the place?"

I admitted I'd been there a few times. Then this Jonas launched into his family tree, wondering if I knew this son of his or that. Maybe there was one or two or all of them I'd heard of, but I kept playing coy.

Then he went through his daughters, ending with the youngest one, named Mary. She was living not far from Peoli. From the gist of his talk, I got the impression she'd been seeing a fellow in our community, but Jonas didn't know much about him. The fellow's name was Eli Beachy, and from what Jonas had heard, he was a no-account guy.

I didn't need eyes in the back of my head to know all my associates were looking at me. I didn't need to be a mind reader to tell you what was being thought, either. That wasn't my concern right then. All I was worried about was surviving to another sunset.

"Say," this elderly Jonas said to me, "I didn't get your name."

"It's Mose Yoder," I said back, not blinking an eye.

Not too long after that, our driver was ready to head for home. We all said our good-byes, piled in the van, and were off. I sat in the first row of seats, thanking my lucky stars in one thought and wondering if anybody was going to say anything in the next. We must have gone thirty miles toward home before the ax fell.

"Hey, Eli," Andy said from the seats behind me, "don't you know that telling a lie is a sin?"

"Yep."

"Hey, Eli, you know that Jonas' Mary?"

"Yep."

"Hey, Eli, you that guy he was talking about?"

"Yep."

"Hey, Eli, you're not half as dumb as I thought."

"Nope."

As the van rolled toward home, I found myself recounting one story after another for the enjoyment of the loafers. As I wove a thin thread of truth through each saga, I knew I had become a man of respect, admired for my creativity as well as my storytelling ability. Until my dying day, I will be remembered as the man who, while teetering on the edge of disaster, thought fast enough to live to tell another story.

Yes, I fibbed that my name was Mose Yoder. Yes, I'd fibbed a time or two to Mary. All things considered, I can't make the promise I'll never fib again. After all, if Jonas ever figures out. . . . Well, it's not a pretty sight, seeing a man dragged down the road behind a buggy. Not saying that he would, but neither am I going to take chances.

10

Propping Up

Choose not alone a proper mate. . . .
—William Cowper

I have reached the conclusion that Amish women are very happy as wives and mothers. Being so happy, they figure that all their unmarried friends must be unhappy. It is therefore the duty of these married ladies to cure this misery. You might call it matchmaking, but we know it as *propping up.*

Now I'm not going to name any names, but Freeman and Mary are good friends of mine up in Holmes County. Good enough friends that I was invited to their family reunion two years ago last July.

I have no problem with such gatherings, for they reflect a favorite hobby of mine: genealogy. Like all the Plain People, we've got quite a chart showing our pedigree. I had no problem in accepting this invitation either, even though hindsight proved something different.

On that Saturday, bright and early, I got a ride up to Freeman's. We visited a bit over coffee, hitched the horse to the buggy, and off we all went. Bell, Freeman's buggy horse, isn't the fastest thing these days, so it took about an hour to cover the five miles to the park.

Once we got to the reunion, Amish social order took over. Freeman's boys took care of parking the horse and buggy. Mary and the girls took care of the food. Freeman and I joined all the other fellows, sitting and talking.

After about half an hour, it was the women's turn to come over and check me out. The first thing one said was "Why didn't you bring your wife and children?"

When I told her I wasn't married, she said, "Oh, how strange."

I happened to glance at Mary, who was blushing, but it didn't bother me. It didn't bother me for about ten minutes, not until Freeman let out with a "Oh, look, here comes our neighbor, Widow Miller."

Sure enough, here a thirty-year-old-or- so lady came across the way, toting her picnic basket. She made a line straight for Freeman's table, put that basket down right across from me, and said, "It's nice to meet you, Eli. Freemans have told me all about you."

I said, "That's very nice. They didn't say a word about you to me."

It was all right though, and I did survive the encounter. I was reminded of that pleasant day about two weeks later. In the margin of my letter from Freeman, in delicate handwriting, was "We always enjoy reading your letters. We are sure there are others who would like to hear from you as well."

That was no big thing. I was going to Freeman's for a visit the next weekend. After a Saturday morning of helping the boys in the field, I wasn't amazed to see an extra buggy at Freeman's hitching post. What a surprise it wasn't to go into the house and extend my greetings.

We had a pleasant dinner there, and after a little visiting, I was kind enough to ride with Arlene back to her home. I returned to Freeman's within twenty minutes, long before he expected me, but Mary already had this one figured out.

Just before supper, I thought it best to put on my Sunday clothes. About halfway through the meal, I mentioned that I thought I'd go out for a walk that evening.

"Great," chimed Freeman. "I'll go with you. That way I can show you where these people live, all the ones you met at the reunion."

There was a great, long silence, and then the distant sound of Mary's shoe connecting to Freeman's shin. She scowled at him and then smiled at me and then scowled at him. Finally the big Amishman realized that he'd better stay home and fix the window before it broke or something.

Sure enough, at a crossroads just out of sight, there was a buggy waiting. As I reflect back on all the fun the Amish can have, let us end this saga by saying that it was a great relief to be invited to Arlene Miller's wedding last year as a guest, not a participant. They sure tried though.

11

Congregations

Brothers and sisters . . . for eternity.
—Eli R. Beachy

Ignorance doesn't kill you,
but it makes you sweat a lot.
—Haitian proverb

It is the work ethic that gives the Amish integrity. The enjoyment of simple fun provides an appreciation of life's simple pleasures. Beyond that, though, there is a cement that bonds the community together. It is simply the congregation, the church group. Here, in the self-imposed backwardness, one finds a society of believers and brothers and sisters, not for an hour or a week, but for eternity.

What dumbfounds most folks is that the Bible and the basic theology of the Amish are the same as that of Methodists, Baptists, or any other Protestant faith. They have to be because the Amish are some of the earliest Protestants. The Lutherans, followers of Martin Luther, came first, but if you look close, the Mennonites and Amish Mennonites weren't far behind.

It's not their basic beliefs but their interpretation and application of them that draws the Amish out of the pack.

The Plain People take great stock in not being worldly. We don't dress differently or do things differently in order to stand out from the crowd. We want to stand away from the crowds. It's not that electricity or the car are sinful, but what they can bring into a home is. We'd far prefer to stay away from that and take support from each other.

To understand the congregation, you need to see all those baptized men and women as a base, a rock that the church is built on—all in agreement and all in support. From this base the leadership of the church is drawn.

A scholar of organizations would have an easy chart to draw if he'd come and study our church. At the top is our bishop, then three preachers, the deacon, and then the congregation. If it seems simple, there's a good reason for that. It is.

Like all Amish congregations, we live by the adage that if you want to keep your holy men humble, don't pay them much. If that be true, Amish churchmen are the humblest on earth because we don't pay them at all. Andy, the one at the mill, is our bishop. Among the preachers we've got a carpenter, a roofer, and a farmer. Our deacon is retired, but nobody ever retires from serving our Lord. These are lifetime hobbies, as it were, performed with a cheerful heart.

Just because this is the way we do it down Peoli way doesn't mean that's the way it is in Baltic or Plain City or elsewhere. You might find two congregations sharing a bishop here, a congregation with just two preachers there. That's because there's no such thing as a conference or association of all Amish churches. The last time I checked, there were 223 congregations in Ohio alone. That makes for a possibility of 223 ways of doing things. It's not that bad, but at times it's not far from it.

One of the funny things I hear English say is that Amish is Amish, they're all the same, and all the horse-and-buggy crowd is one big happy family. In actuality there have been eleven schisms since 1910 among Ohio's Amish. A bishop, or bishops, will take exception to the norm, lead a flock out on their own thinking, and a new branch of the Amish tree is formed. With just a few exceptions, these offshoots are named for the bishop or for their locale.

Most folks have heard of the Old Order Amish, and they are the most common. Some also know of the New Order Amish, the ones on rubber-rimmed buggy wheels. A few are even aware of the Swartzentruber Amish, the conservative ones. Sometimes I think it's sad how little folks do know. Other times, it's just as well they don't end up as confused as we can get.

If you made a list of the Amish styles in Ohio, you'd have to include King, Dan Miller, New Order, Old Order, Chesterhill, Tobe Hostettler, Andy Weaver, Roman Miller, Stutzman Troyers, Swartzentruber, Sam Yoder, and, last but not least, the bottom of the barrel, Peoli. That's not us, that's our neighbors. But more on that later.

Here are twelve factions that are no more than parameters within which those 223 congregations fit. Just because one Old Order congregation does things one way doesn't mean every one does. The factions dress differently, have different buggy accessories, and accept different degrees of technology. It's absolutely a confusion, even to the buggy crowd. One thing for sure comes out of this mess. If you ever hear somebody saying this is the way the Amish do something, lumping us all together, you know he doesn't know what he's talking about.

Noah and I went to a town not long ago where a woman

was giving a speech about the Amish. The people in charge of the program said it was all right if we sat in, as long as we didn't say anything. They didn't want us to start a commotion. I couldn't understand that warning until I heard the woman talk.

She spoke for over an hour, and I think I heard her get three things right. Noah got fed up with the stupidity of it and left, but I stuck it out, figuring it would get better. I made it all the way up to where she said that the quaintest Amish are the Swartzentrubers. Back home we've got another name for them. We call them hillbillies.

I don't mean to be going off on a tangent, but I've held back long enough. There's some people I just can't get along with, and our hillbilly neighbors are some of them. I don't mean to be better than anybody and try to be humbler than most. It just irritates me to no end that some not only think that all Amish are the same, but also that we're all a bunch of friends.

There's some kin of mine in this bunch, but I'm not proud of it. From Easter to Thanksgiving, they're all going barefoot. Their farms are pigpens, and they themselves are untidy. Whereas the Amish in general average seven children, this bunch averages twelve. They're out at night without a slow-moving vehicle sign. They speak English rarely, and some think it's still 1800. Others haven't even caught up to that time yet.

Peoli Joseph, one of them, was once going to be a farmer. One summer they were working as a threshing crew. Somehow the machine got jammed. Joseph jumped back there to free it, and when it came clear, the bar came down and severed his leg.

They rushed around, some running over to get the

neighbors to come and others pouring kerosene over Joe's leg. Believe it or not, the kerosene's not too bad. It has a soothing effect and does prevent shock. At any rate, only a few minutes later the neighbor arrived in his truck.

They rushed off to Memorial Hospital, but they couldn't reattach his leg. The best the doctors could do was get Joe stabilized. When the family was sure he'd be all right, they loaded him up with his severed leg and went home.

This bunch then proceeded to go out to the family cemetery and bury Joe's leg. They believe that if you do that the victim will be free from the pain that comes with amputation. The problem was, Joe still had pain.

They went out, dug the leg up, turned it over, and reburied it. Joe doesn't have any more pain, but you don't need to think that I care to associate with people like that, either.

Just when I thought I'd seen everything, it must have been fate that led me along that back road the first week of November. Considering the time of year, the weather was fairly pleasant. It was a good thing, the sun shining and all, because this good weather allowed me to savor an absolute circus.

This wasn't Ringling Brothers three-ring tent, but people would probably pay to have an act like this one. It would be far too simple just to say the clowns in this show were Swartzentruber Peolis, and write it off to their peculiarities. No, this one was a spectacular to be savored, and it needs to be told.

When I got there, a team of four good-looking Percherons was tied via a chain to a one-room shed. I'd say, judging by the skid marks, they'd dragged the shed from right by the roadway, through the yard, and around the barn to

where I saw it. When I saw it, the shed was so stuck on the side of a dirt mound that it might never move off.

Even though they were Swartzentruber Peolis, they were still people in need, so I stopped. Right into a hornet's nest I walked. The three young fellows, sons of the farm, were so mad they couldn't even talk—furious, neck-vein-bulging mad. When I got the story of what was going on from their dad, I think I could see why.

Every year Jake, the man of the house, likes to grow melons to sell. He uses this shed as a roadside stand. Every April he drags it from the barn to the roadside and hangs out a shingle. Every November he drags it back, through the yard, around the barn. And for the past five years, he has gotten it stuck on the same dirt mound.

Jake was absolutely dumbfounded when I asked him why they didn't level off the dirt mound before the dragging began. He looked at me like it was an idea that had never occurred to him. Obviously the thought had passed through the boys' minds. I could feel their blood pressures, already at the boiling point, just about ready to go into orbit.

It was an ideal time to be moving on, before any more great revelations came my way. I wound my way on home, chuckling the whole way. By the time I made it through our back door, I was absolutely hysterical with laughter. What a discovery I'd made. We're living just up the way from the first Amish pea-brains.

I was still laughing about this clown when I stopped over to see Mervin for a few minutes. Those Peolis are really something, and I'm glad I don't have too much to do with them. I figured Mervin would appreciate it, him doing some business with them from time to time.

Appreciate it he did, getting some chuckle out of my account of the exploit. When I was all done, he laughed and then had me repeat this clown's name. Without another word, Mervin went over to his bookcase and pulled out a paperback called *Die Kalender.*

Die Kalender is really our almanac. It's got that zodiac mumbo-jumbo and the witty sayings, but more too. There's an outline in there for each month's church services, reminding us what Scriptures will be read and hymns sung. That's all well and good, but it was the last section that Mervin found most interesting.

Those pages list the bishops, preachers, and deacons for congregations across the country. Mervin thumbed through until he found the right page. He ran his finger along the print until he found what he wanted. Giving me a sickening grin, he motioned for me to take a look at what he found.

I said I don't like those people and don't want anything to do with them. I don't know much about them, and until that moment, could not have cared less. Even without looking at the print, somehow I knew what coming.

What about the dumb guy, the one called Jake? Among that crowd, they call him Bishop Jake.

Those size sevens of mine are getting quite comfortable in my mouth these days.

I'll grant you that I bad-mouth this bunch more than I should. I hold my opinions too long as well. I just don't want to get too close, or too downwind. Just to show there's no truly hard feelings, I even do business with one of them. Just one, but it's a start.

I spend most Friday mornings arguing with the Swartzentruber Peoli fellow running a local sawmill. One morning Abe said to me, "Eli, if some stranger would hear us talk, they just might get the wrong impression. When two men chew on each other this much, some others get to thinking they're the best of friends. I'd just hate to have the neighbors thinking we actually like each other."

So would I, especially since I do consider Abe a great friend. Who knows? I might even invite him over to the house sometime. It's really something going through life being wrong, but I'm not above admitting it—someday.

12

Rules

What I do today, I sleep with tonight.
—Eli R. Beachy

A man cannot be comfortable
without his own approval.
—Mark Twain

Thinking about those neighbors got me so upset that I strayed way off course. We were talking about the organization of the Amish church, the bishop on down to the body of believers known as the congregation. Even though I mentioned that all the holy positions were a lifetime calling, one thing I've neglected is our somewhat unique selection process known as the *lot*.

Suppose one of our preachers passed away. At the next communion service, which is held once in the spring and once in fall, the wheels start turning to select a new man. Using a combination of democracy and divine intervention, the congregation will make sure of its survival.

The election will be held with all baptized members of the congregation voting, men and women alike. Should a man receive three or more votes, he's placed into what's called the lot. Once the lot is assembled, at the same service, that group will retire to another room, where there is a Bible for each man. After prayer, each man in the lot will select a Bible as the Spirit moves him, and if the Bible chosen has a single piece of paper slipped in it, that man has become the new Amish preacher.

Things were done different around here until just a short time ago. We had a unique custom regarding the lot, not waiting until the next communion but getting right on with it as soon as possible. I never gave it much thought, figuring if we'd done it that way for a long time, it must be all right.

As a matter of fact, I was one of the last to agree that a change would be appropriate. Simply changing for the sake of something different never has set well with me. Just because most, if not all, Amish congregations select a replacement leader at the next communion was a fine reason, but not fine enough for me. I might have stayed firm against the revision but for a visit from Old John, the deacon of our church.

John came calling in the spirit of friendship and to give me a history lesson. The Amish who first came to Ohio landed in the Holmes County area. The community grew, spreading out from time to time. Some reached Plain City before the turn of the century; others were up in Geauga County. Our people didn't start showing up in this neck of the woods until about 1950.

I was born here and always figured it was just a nice place some folks found and took to one day. Listening to John talk about old times gave me clues that those were less-than-ideal times. He remembered firsthand and figured I'd like to hear about some things that haven't been discussed much now in forty years.

During World War II and for a few years afterward, some county officials up north believed it their duty to force Amish children into public schools. It got really ugly, with some Amish parents being put in jail and their children placed into foster homes. Noah Hershberger of Wisconsin even wrote a book about the whole situation, *Struggle to Be Separate*. I've read that text and would recommend it in a second, but I never dreamed the school problem caused us to be here on the Peoli Road.

When I read that book, like many others hereabouts, I formed a dual opinion on an underlying factor that started off this controversy. Certainly it could be true, and we hope that it is, that those county officials were just doing their job. Given the public trust, they were simply interpreting the letter of the law. That reasoning is far preferable to another logic, which notes that 1944 just happened to be the year when the prosecutions began.

History says that was in the middle of a popular war for people of these United States. The Amish stood in the middle of all this war fervor, conscientious objectors to the use of violence to resolve any conflict. Perhaps some officials, when given the public trust, chose to punish those who didn't march off to the so-called glory of killing another human being.

Some Americans became confused and lumped conscientious objectors (COs) with deserters. We serve, but not in combat or combat-related duties. An obligation to fulfill to this great country is not a problem for the pleasure of living in the United States. I suppose some don't understand others' beliefs, and maybe they don't try to, either.

I was drafted during the Vietnam conflict, but unlike so many others, I thought it was a good idea. I went to a CO outfit, doing hospital work. Funny as it may seem, I met all sorts of fellows who were COs as long as any chance of being killed in that war existed. Once the shooting stopped, their peacefulness went right out the window. Well, we Amish don't work that way. We live our conviction every day. That's our business, to live a life not on convenience but righteousness. Those semipeace fellows might not ever understand that. They thought me wanting to be in service was absolute insanity.

Yet I was happy to be changing linens and bedpans eight hours a day. I labored hard, but not for the pay or for the veteran's benefits I never claimed. It was for the next eight hours after each shift of work. That eight hours all of us from a buggy community spent watching television.

These thoughts came racing back to me as Deacon John kept talking about the court cases, fines, and judgments levied against the Amish in those days. There was a lot of fear as the 1940s came to a close. That fear brought our bunch down this way. Our group hoped that, with some miles between here and all that trouble, cooler heads just might prevail.

All of a sudden, John's words made a lot of sense. Our congregation had lived in fear of a modern persecution for forty years. We'd ordained holy men as soon as possible to represent us in case the law come knocking. I came to understand that our recent tradition of fast ordination was for protection. As I recalled how good English people have been to us around here, I knew those bad days were behind us. With no reason to be looking over our shoulders any more, I told John I'd be voting to bring us into line with everybody else on this policy the next Sunday.

This notion of a vote and then Bible selection within the

lot is the same process by which a deacon is selected. It runs true for selecting a bishop as well, except that there's no vote by the congregation. The lot for bishop has already been determined, limited to the current preachers of the congregation. One of those two, three, or four will be taking the job.

The possibility of the lot falling on a member so unpredictably is one of many reasons all Amish are up on their Bible study at all times. Being ordained is a tremendous responsibility, not to be shirked. There has yet to be a man return from the lot who didn't comment that the heart was pounding but the hands were cool.

A lot of people get confused and think the authority of the congregation rests solely with these men. That's not really the way it is. These fellows simply make sure the body of believers stays as one within a set of rules the congregation, not the bishops or anybody else, has decided on.

Twice a year, spring and fall, Amish congregations meet and confirm their rules for living. That's the *Ordnung* that's been mentioned before. It's a rare time that change slips in. Believe it or not, some in the United States are quite happy as they are.

Ordnungs are complete, covering a lot of ground. The rules are set for clothing, what technology is acceptable, buggy style, even down to household furnishings. There's nothing left to doubt by the time the congregation, in a unanimous vote, approves another six months of structure.

Just because there are a lot of rules doesn't mean the Amish are so rigid that they can't breathe. The *Ordnung* is like a fence around a field. We're the field, the Good Word is the seed. If we stay in the fence and let our brotherhood cultivate the good and thrive under the light of our Lord, things have a habit of working out just fine.

However, there is one small problem with such a complete set of rules. We saw this with the television incident involving Mary and her iron. Once a set of rules like a congregation's *Ordnung* are made crystal clear, then there are also exceptions to those rules.

I've got cousins in a congregation near Mount Hope, and it's real clear there. Ever since anybody can remember, their *Ordnung* has clearly stated that they cannot have electrical wires come into the home, aren't permitted to own a telephone, and in no way are to own a mechanically powered vehicle.

Those are the rules, and, yes, indeed, that's what they live with. You'll not find an electric wire running from the road to Ben's buildings, but instead you would find a portable generator to run those power tools of Ben's and that Hoover vacuum of Amanda's. The phone company owns the pay phone on the corner of their lot, not them. But that's nothing compared to what I saw last July when I was in Walnut Creek.

Here came Ben driving a fairly new pickup truck right into the gasoline station. Not riding in it, *driving* it. It was against my better judgment, but I had to go over and find out what was going on.

"Hey, I don't own it," said Ben. "I lease it."

I'm sure there are Baptists, Methodists, Jews, and probably Muslims pulling the same stunt. Religion is great, just as long as it stays convenient.

The way I see it, the own-versus-lease option on that pickup is an issue for Ben's conscience. What I do today, I sleep with tonight. Up to now, for forty-plus years, I've been a sound sleeper, and I plan to keep it that way.

13

Making Ready

*Then it was bucket-of-water, on-your-knees-scrubbing,
corner-cleaning time.*
—Eli R. Beachy

Ivan claims we all go to church all the time because
there's no collection plate. That might be true for some, but
the majority really do take to such a gathering. Everybody
must enjoy this, especially when you consider how different this gathering can be. Amish church runs about four
hours every other Sunday. Like so much else with our people, the four hours and the every other Sunday is a matter
of tradition, just the way we've always done it. Throw in
the fact that those four hours are on a backless bench, and
I don't think too many outsiders care for such an uncom-
fortable religion.

The ideal size for an Amish congregation must be
twenty-six families. That way each homeplace could have
church once a year. Around here we're just beyond perfect,
with thirty-two families now in our area and church making its full circle in about fourteen months.

It was our turn to hold the gathering last month. I knew
it but didn't give it a lot of thought until that Tuesday before the Sunday service. When I got in from pounding

nails that evening, I saw Deacon John had been by with the green box wagon, and it was time to set to work on the home front.

The green wagon is how we get church supplies from one site to the next. All John does is pick it up from last week's locale and drive it over to the next place of worship. It was left to me, the homeowner, to unload the folding benches and boxes of hymnals and then load them back up the week after services. That would be fine if that's all there was to it. Having Amish church requires a lot more, let me tell you.

The first order of business was for us to get all the furniture out of the way to make space. Then it was bucket-of-water, on-your-knees-scrubbing, corner-cleaning time. If it couldn't be cleaned with the scrub brush, then it was run through the washing machine. If not washed, then it was painted. The next few days were definitely not the time to be coming in the back door with muddy boots.

Not until Saturday had the house reached that spotless stage where I could start hauling in the benches. We've got eighty of them in our wagon. I unloaded each one, carried it into the house, unfolded its legs, and placed it. This may not sound like much, and if I had a full day to do it all, it wouldn't be. The problem was, I had to rush. Arranging the benches was one more afternoon chore to prepare for a church meeting at our place.

I imagine the grocery store down toward town loves it when the Amish get together for fellowship. We were not only having services, we were also expected to feed the group. So I found myself almost cleaning out some of their shelves. Sixty pounds of chunk baloney, thirty pounds of Swiss cheese, thirty-five loaves of bread, three cases of pickles, and fifteen pounds of coffee later, and I was headed for home with the sun going down. Unfortunately, the work wasn't done yet.

It was well after midnight before the last of the baloney had been sliced up and everything else was ready. All this work's not for me. I'd far prefer to be tired from raising a barn every day than from all these chores. Still, for the chance to fellowship with our community, our people, it's well worth it.

The warm weather had come our way. With the windows open and a pleasant breeze flowing, it felt downright comfortable sitting on that pew the next morning. I felt peaceful and relaxed as Andy launched into the main sermon. Funny how just a few minutes into it, all his words seemed to jumble together for me.

If my head would have fallen so my chin was on my chest, there might not have been any problem. Some claim it was pure chance, while I think I had some help, but it's still a fact that my head went back instead. As it went back, my mouth fell open and the snoring started and even got louder as Andy preached, so I was told.

To his credit, Andy delivered one of the most memorable benedictions in the history of our congregation. His words were so memorable that they, or Ivan's elbow in my ribs, roused me from the depths of slumber and left a lasting impression in my mind.

"Sometimes the Word of God is meant to inspire us. Other times it can give us rest. Whichever it be, may each and every one not have to stay up too late getting ready for church. Amen."

Amen is right to that one.

14

Contentment

Preach the gospel always. If necessary, use words.
—Francis of Assissi

There are a few good books floating around that can clue you in on the particulars of how an Amish service is operated. I thumbed through some by Scott, finding myself nodding along with what he shared. He can write well, better than I, to tell you how a hymn from the *Ausbund* or *Liedersammlung* can last for thirty minutes. How the deacon reads not a verse or two, but whole chapters of Scripture. What they can't tell you is what happens when you get a windy preacher.

Services down home had been stretching closer to five hours than four when Preacher Ben came to see Deacon John up the way. It was obvious, even from the start, that Ben was concerned that he might be carrying on too long.

At the same time, it was just as obvious that John wasn't going to speak his piece. After all, he was dealing with the Word of God. Back and forth they went, Ben wanting to hear John's opinion, and John not wanting to step on toes, especially the Lord's.

Finally, in exasperation, Preacher Ben said, "John, I do not mind if a man takes out his pocket watch to check the time. What I do mind is when he takes it out, checks the time, and then shakes it to see if it's still running. Don't do that anymore!"

It's been noted among the congregation that the preaching has been shorter of late. John, he just smiles, but he also doesn't bring his watch to church anymore, either.

About five miles northwest of here is a Mennonite church. They're our cousins, not in terms of blood but in faith. The Amish are the more conservative offshoot of the religious heritage, but there's a lot more to it than that.

If the notion of different factions of the Amish tends to confuse, then the study of the Mennonites would absolutely dumbfound. There are fourteen different conferences, or governing bodies, of Mennonites in Ohio today. Then there are the Conservative Mennonites, divided between conference members and independents. There are also Amish Mennonites, often called Beachy Amish, floating around. Throw in the one bunch of horse-and-buggy Old Order Mennonites which you find north of Mansfield, and you've got a real jumble.

Just like with the Amish, all these folks operate under the same Scripture and the same basic belief as any other Protestant faith. It's in the interpretation and application of the faith where all the differences show up. Some Mennonite women don't wear prayer caps while other factions look downright Amish except when they drive cars.

Some scholars focus on the car as that signifying break between Mennonite and Amish, although there were no cars in 1693 when the break first occurred. Others point to education, noting that most of the Mennonites support higher learning while we're limited to basic schooling.

Many count electricity as the determining boundary. Historians say the split was chiefly over Amish shunning or avoiding excommunicated members. Certainly each point has its merits to help in understanding the difference, but around here we might be onto something even more identifying about the Mennonites.

Dave's a feed salesman who stops in at the mill about once a month or so. He belongs to that Mennonite church in our end of the county. For a young fellow, he's pretty sharp, being well versed on the history of both the Mennonites and his congregation.

Oftentimes, especially in Holmes and Wayne counties, Mennonite churches have a large percentage of former Amish in their membership. That's not the case with our neighbors. Not a single one born in an Amish home is on the roster. From what Dave told us, more than half the church had converted from another faith to being Mennonite. Even the pastor had started out as a Lutheran before coming over.

Around here, we see that sense of evangelism as the real dividing line between the Amish and the Mennonites. With representatives like Dave, their church is spreading the Good Word wherever they can find a listener. The Mennonites witness, testify, are missionaries, and just plain evangelize around the world. They're steadily growing in this country and spreading like wildfire in what some call the developing countries, wherever that might be.

Dave was pretty serious with us all at the mill when he stopped in. He was telling us that each of us should be spreading the Word. I was sitting there on the sacks of dog food, listening until he was just about finished. Then I said, "I'm not much for being the evangelist, Dave."

"Oh, yes, you are, Eli," he said, turning to face me. "You're an evangelist even if you don't know it. You evangelize with your appearance, your buggy, and by being a people apart. You evangelize, yes, you do."

I shook my head and said, "No, Dave, I'm not an evangelist, I'm an example." I heard Andy muttering something about liking to make an example out of me, but I didn't pay any attention. Instead, I let that sink in for a minute before I went on.

"Do you know that I, personally, don't believe in God, Dave?"

His eyes bulged out in shock at such a heathen remark, but I held my hand up to hold the floor.

"I don't believe," I went on, "because I know. I can see the Lord in every blade of grass, every sunrise, every rainstorm, every single thing. That's a contented feeling to wake up with.

"It's also contentment to know there are others feeling just like I do. They not only feel like me, but are willing to be there should anyone, anyone, need a hand. We trust each other enough to depend on them, and there's not too much else you can ask of a man.

"There's a contentment in living my life, the only life I've ever known, the way I'm comfortable with. Living in peace, you don't have to be wrong for me to be right. I don't force anything on you, and you give me the same privilege. That's a good feeling too.

"I don't force my life on anyone but, should they ask about what they see, I'll answer. Some do, and one question leads to another. Once in a while, after enough questions, one person of the world becomes one of our people. Rare, but it happens. This is a life at one with nature, one with peace, one with fellow humans, and one with our Lord, all for the asking. Few do cross over to become Amish, but maybe those are the ones prepared to hear the answers."

It was quiet for a bit in the mill that day. You could tell Dave was thinking of all the arguments he could toss back. You could also see him rebutting each as soon as he thought of it. It took a minute or two before a twinkle came to his eyes.

"Eli, if you ever get tired of riding around in a buggy, the Mennonites sure could use a persuasive preacher like you."

I felt the twinkle coming to my eyes as I said, "If you ever get tired of that electricity, I'll be right here waiting for you."

15

The Things We Do for Money

*That rare bird we've identified as the
rubber-necked arm-flinger.*
—Eli R. Beachy

*I'm opposed to millionaires,
but it would be dangerous
to offer me the position.*
—Mark Twain

Problems like having a windy preacher are really small
potatoes compared to struggles of some people. Clumps of
Amish families are moving out of state because the farmland we all cherish isn't available, at least at a good price.
Only one in three Amish is farming today, and that's an
issue we discuss. If you look real close, more of that migration out of here is caused by those rare birds we've identified as the rubber-necked arm-flingers, whom you know as
tourists.

We don't have it too bad down home, but we pity our
Holmes County cousins. I may not be popular with some
of them, but up that way, a number of the English are taking advantage of their Amish neighbors and of the tourists
too. It's a matter of time until more than the Amish get
ticked off about what the county puts out and the state of
Ohio promotes.

If you think I'm off base, maybe you'd better take a look at that county's tourist information. Last time I looked, of the nearly one hundred places listed, less than ten were Amish-owned. The housewife, the farmer, the carpenter, and the mason who happen to be Amish can't even get to town for business on the weekend anymore. You can be assured that they appreciate it less than I do.

Maybe it all comes down to the Amish not having any public relations fellow spreading the news. Somebody hears, or somebody says, and the next thing you know, it's a fact. Sometime those facts are even news to the Amish.

We were down to Ammon's not long ago, pretending we were state workers. There were five of us standing around watching him paint his gate. Up the road came a car.

The best thing Ohio ever did was to put county stickers on the license plates. You can spot a stranger a mile away, and this one was from Cleveland. He looked over, jammed on the brakes, stopped the car, jumped out, and ran over.

"Is it true?" he asked.

"Could be," I said. "What's that?"

He said, "I heard that when an Amishman paints his gate blue, he's got an eligible daughter."

"Yes, sir, that could well be," I answered.

That made this fellow as happy as a clam. He jumped back in his car, and off he went. Ammon kept on painting until the car was out of sight. Then he turned around, threw down his brush, and shook his head.

"Why did you lie to him?" Ammon asked.

"I didn't," I responded. "I just didn't finish my sentence. It could be true . . . but I think not."

Ammon has ten sons. One may be a bit peculiar, but no girls ever came along at his house.

Ammon was painting his gate blue for a good reason, though. He was painting his gate blue for the same reason Jake painted his blue. The same reason Levi painted his blue and I'll paint mine the same color. Blue was on sale at K Mart a month ago, and we all stocked up.

Saving money has always been a high priority item for Ammon. I'm not saying he's as cheap as Old Weaver, but Ammon tends to the frugal way. He was always running off to the store to buy something on sale, whether he needed it or not. From there he's usually off to the bank, putting all those nickels and dimes away.

That's all well and good, since Ammon was certainly not wasting any gasoline on these jaunts. But several of us did comment on his means of transportation. That old buggy horse of his, now pushing thirty-five years old, couldn't be making too many more miles. Ammon always figured there was one more mile left in that chestnut mare, so it was no worry to him. No worry at least until that one Tuesday we remember so well.

One of the best additions to the banking industry has to be the addition of the drive-up windows. You don't have to hunt for a parking place anymore. Just pull right in line and take care of business. One Tuesday, that was exactly what Ammon was up to, making a deposit down in town at the bank there.

He'd just finished his transaction when that buggy horse let out with a shudder and proceeded to die right there in the drive-through lane. Some say it was a heart attack, but I don't know that that matters. There were several more candidates for heart failure right about then. Nobody had ever had a horse die at the bank before.

Everybody rushed around for a while, wondering what

to do. Finally somebody thought to go across the street to the gas station. They've got a wrecker truck there, and sure enough, they were happy to lend a hand. They weren't going to haul it to the rendering plant, but at least they would clear the lane.

All this excitement happened around noontime as the bank president was having his lunch down at the Lamplight Inn. He came strolling up the street about one, just like he always does. He might have noticed the buggy parked in his lot. He probably noticed Ammon, sitting under the maple tree, waiting for the truck from the rendering plant. One thing for sure, judging by his yelling, he did notice a dead horse lying in the bank's front yard.

Since the carcass truck would be along soon, it really didn't bother Ammon. It sure didn't bother the gas station people, either, them being a payment or two behind to the bank anyway. It certainly did upset that bank president, judging by the way he ripped and tore there for a while.

Some say he was shouting that he wasn't going to allow any more buggies at the bank and other thoughtless comments. Fortunately, his assistant got out some folders to remind the boss of a few things. Something about how the Plain People deposits at that bank didn't total tens of thousands, but hundreds of thousands.

Just like that, all the anger was gone from Mr. President. Reminded of the value of a dollar, the bank's leader was soon seen outside with his arm around Ammon's shoulders, regretting the unfortunate death and wondering if Ammon ever considered financing his next four-footed purchase.

Ah, the things we do for money.

16

The English

*Life was meant to be lived,
and curiosity must be kept alive.*
—Anna Eleanor Roosevelt

Sometimes even those Hollywood movie people have been known to get into the act of telling about the Plain People. One of the latest intrusions into the Amish world was a movie called *Witness*. We don't go for the worldly amusements, but we were by a neighbor's place awhile back. They're English and have a television and one of those VCR things. They started the film after we got there, so it was just neighborly to hang around and watch.

To be honest, it was a pretty good film about Pennsylvania. I didn't see any need for the violence. And the adult situations, I decided after I'd watched them three or four times, were out of place, but not bad. What was really surprising was that it wasn't what I thought of as a Hollywood movie.

If I were going to do something and put a Hollywood label on it, I'd make it Hollywood. Instead of having an Amish boy witness a murder in a big city, I'd have an Amishman commit the terrible deed on the farm. He would murder his wife, take her out to the barn, and then burn it down around her, claiming she had a heart attack.

To keep the same title, there is a witness. It would be this fellow's hired man, another Amishman who lives by the principle that you don't go around judging others so that you're not judged yourself (Matthew 7:1). He'll never testify, living his life with a remembrance too horrible to speak of or to forget.

As the truth is revealed, our villain killed his wife because he's really a homosexual. On the farm he next gets involved with drinking, then drugs. Finally he leaves the area, goes off to the Southwest, commits another murder, is caught and put away for a long time.

Now isn't that Hollywood? It appears to be the product of a vivid imagination. So vivid that you might find yourself with an Amish frame of mind, hoping that Eli, the son of an Amish holy man, is never released from a Texas jail. Sometimes real life is much crazier than Hollywood.

That story has floated around the town of Kidron for some years now. Seemed like each time we'd go up there for the Thursday auction, there'd be someone or another adding a detail or two. With almost everybody talking, it seemed strange that there was one crowd that said nothing. It just seemed to me that if you were a Stutzman-Troyer Amish, you kept your mouth shut; you just might know more than the rest of us.

The sale barn there is the only place I've ever seen the Stutzman-Troyers. I've heard some say there's only one congregation of them and their corduroy coats in Ohio. All the rest moved to New York State. I don't see any problem if they stay up that way, I stay here, and things will stay just fine.

I wouldn't say I'm a bigot, but I do offend easily. I'm

sure others have the same problem, dealing with zealots. We always figured this bunch spent a lot of time trying to outchurch everybody else. I'm offended by anybody's holier-than-thou attitude. And one other small point. I don't think this crowd has seen the bathtub too many more times than our Peoli neighbors.

Still, this is the greatest country in the world. We've got no problem paying our taxes for the pleasure of being Americans. That's why, this being such a great country, it troubled us when we heard there were so many poor people in the United States.

It bothered us so much that Noah and I hitched up the buggy and went to town. We made a beeline right to the library and started to research the issue. It didn't take long to determine exactly where that poverty line was, and we're sorry we did.

When we determined where the line was, we discovered we were beneath it; we're poor people, too. All this time we were under an unpoor notion and quite happy, thank you. We've consoled ourselves with the knowledge that it's no sin to live in poverty. It is a bit unhandy though.

Maybe poverty was the problem the last time I was in Berlin. Against my better judgment, I was in town tourist-watching. Right in the middle of uptown was a big tour bus. Judging by what happened, it must have been loaded with poor people.

The bus door opened and a couple got off, man and woman. They went right over to the hitching post. She grabbed a stick and started poking around. Next thing you know, he took one of those styrofoam coffee cups out of his pocket.

My tale is as true as I am here: they proceeded to load

up that cup with horse droppings. He popped the vented lid on it, and they trotted right back on the bus. Can you imagine what it smelled like to ride back to Pittsburgh with somebody too cheap to spend two dollars to buy the stuff in a sealed plastic bag? Tourists.

You know, though, our one experience with the tourist business down home has caused some to think. Three months ago, in the height of the heat, tourism found us in a most unusual way.

Jake and Andy, down at the mill, had noticed a car making a circle or two of the building. When they heard the engine stop, they took a peek. There, out back, was a woman rooting through the trash pile. In just a few seconds, she pulled out a chicken crate, and here she came. Into the mill she charged, saying, "I want to buy this."

Something you might have heard is that the language of the Amish home is what's called Pennsylvania Deutsch (Dutch, some say), a dialect of German. When we go to school, we learn English as a foreign language. Sometimes it's inconvenient, and other times like this one, it's a lifesaver.

Jake looked at Andy and in Deutsch said, "Buy? We're throwing that junk away."

Andy nodded, turned to the lady, and in English said, "They're $10."

Poor Jake was choking on that one, especially when the woman wanted to dicker. Jake probably could have used a heart specialist when the price was finally set at $7.50.

Somewhere in the city of Columbus is a very happy woman. Undoubtedly, her living room is decorated with a used, stinking chicken crate. As to Jake and Andy, the last I was to the mill, they were both going through the trash one more time seeing if there was anything else they might be able to sell.

Perhaps all these tourist problems arise because we've gotten spoiled. A family can go on vacation to Williamsburg or Disney World and see actors playing a part for their benefit. Maybe then they end up in Amish country expecting the same.

With forty thousand horse-and-buggy folk spread throughout Ohio, there's bound to be a few who are tourist-curious. I know an Englishman who does a lot of business and traveling in Amish communities. He claims that 25 percent can't stand him, 50 percent can take or leave him, and 25 percent are just as curious about him as he is about them.

I managed to piece together the parts of one story long after it happened. A fellow was coming to see us one day. Being uncertain, he made a wrong turn. All of a sudden, the road he was on led down into a valley. He knew this wasn't right because we live on the ridge.

Fortunately, just ahead was an Amish farm, with the man of the house just coming in from the field. The fellow in the car waved, the farmer waved back, so he stopped for directions.

"Say," the out-of-towner said. "I'm looking for Eli's place."

"Eli's place?" came the answer. The Amish have a habit of repeating a question, not for being ignorant but to conserve breath. They want the answer right the first time.

"If you're looking for Eli's, you're on the wrong road."

The English looked exasperated and said, "I know that!"

This was about the funniest thing the Amishman ever heard. It was so comical that both men had to mosey over to the nearby bench. As they found their positions, the verbal jousting began.

"Eli," the Deutscher went on, "he's quite a carpenter."

It was obvious that the guest already knew that, and that wasn't the purpose of the visit. The Amishman then started grabbing at straws.

"Eli's dad, he was a horse dealer, you know."

The Englishman's stock soared to the moon when he acknowledged he'd heard that, but he'd also heard it was my uncle who was the real horse trader. Back and forth it went, the Englisher wise to our way and not giving an inch. Finally, after checking the license of the car and seeing it was from Columbus, the Amish asked, "From around here?"

Tom, the Englisher, finally decided enough was enough. He clued this fellow in that he was coming to call because of our mutual interest in genealogy. Before the Amishman could draw this one out, the door of the house opened and out came the lady of the farm.

Some say she didn't make any bones about satisfying her curiosity. She made a line to her husband, and in the Deutsch language, asked who this guy was and what he wanted. After checking that Tom didn't understand the lingo, the farmer set his wife straight: Tom was all right.

Just like that, she switched to English and said, "I just come out to tell you the pies are out of the oven."

Of course, it wouldn't be neighborly not to offer a slice of pie to a new friend. Once you have him in the house, then it's just polite to show off your own genealogy. Talk of this, talk of that, and before you knew it, four hours had slipped away.

I didn't say much to Tom when he finally drove in to the homeplace. Somehow I knew he'd had his ear talked out, having found one of those 25 percent English-curious ones. I'd like to claim that I could understand because I'm so perceptive about our neighbors, but there's another reason.

It took my cousin Mervin, the Amishman, four hours to give a set of directions that might have read like "Go to that crossroad fifty feet up there and turn right. If you drive to the top of the hill, you might find that guy Eli, who has been waving to us."

Yet who am I to deny a man his fun?

17

Friends

Come where you belong.
—Jonas Ruth

*A friend is someone who makes
me feel totally acceptable.*
—Ene Riisna

Every once in awhile you might see Amish people riding around in a van. If you're buggy-bound and have to go great distances, that's the preferred means of travel. Hiring a van and driver is not cheap, running to at least forty cents a mile and sometimes more, so you'll always see those vans full. Forty cents a mile split twenty ways is a lot easier on the pocketbook.

The wallet was what I was thinking of when a letter came from far northeast of here about a job for my carpenters. It sounded good, good enough to take a look, but forty cents a mile was going to be costing me too much. After a little thought, I decided to do something wild and to hitchhike.

When I told Mervin, my second in command on the crew, what I was up to, you should have heard him hoot.

"You can't be doing that," he warned me. "There's a lot

of crazy people out driving around these parts."

"I know that," I said. "But there's a lot of crazy people hitchhiking, too."

You could see in Mervin's eyes that he thought I fit that same type. He nodded, accepting the truth in my words, and said, "Have a good trip."

The next morning I got a car-driving neighbor to give me a lift over to the interstate. I was trying to keep a low profile since our people aren't much for hitching rides. Nothing's ever been said, but it's accepting charity, and we're not much for that. It's also getting close to the English world as well. I was still weighing these negatives as I hopped out of Brian's car, got in position, and held up my thumb.

Those who speak of the luck of the Irish are only off by two letters. With the luck of the Amish, within one minute's time I was in the cab of one of those big semi trucks. Not only was he heading in my direction; he was going right past where I wanted to be. It was a quite enjoyable ride, I might note, talking of this and that.

My luck held at the project site as well. It was an easy job, and I put in a bid I thought to be high. Within an hour I was walking back to the roadway, with the signed contract in my pocket and a promise of more business headed our way.

When the second passing truck pulled over to give me a ride toward home, I was thinking I should have been a big-time gambler, with all my luck. I was well pleased to learn that his destination was about two miles from the homeplace. If I'd be willing to wait while he made a few stops on the way, I'd be eating supper right on time.

His errands didn't bother me, but might bother some. I

was riding in the carcass truck, going to different livestock farms, and picking up the dead cattle. Bob was heading for the rendering plant in our neighborhood. I may not care for those people at that plant for a number of reasons, but the ride was convenient.

On the first stop, south of where I'd been, things got interesting. We had just pulled into the livestock barn when an Amishman came walking around the corner. As I've mentioned, whenever two or more Amish join together, good talk breaks out. I hopped out of that truck, and even though I'd never seen this fellow before, talk we did.

His name was Bert, and he seemed to be rather friendly as we loaded a hide into the truck. We talked a little bit before he looked at me and said, "Where you coming from?"

I told him I'd been to Medina County, and he said, "I thought so. Medina County? I know your brother."

I said, "You do?"

"Oh, yes," returned Bert. "He came over from Lodi not long ago. I bought some heifers from him. Good price. You see him, send him back. We can do business."

I nodded that I would and then said, "How do you know that was my brother? You don't even know my name other than Eli."

"Don't kid me," he insisted. "You guys are almost twins. You look alike, talk alike, and there's not too many of us with blue eyes."

The fellow with the truck was ready, so I said my goodbye. We'd gone maybe a mile or two when the driver asked, "What does your brother do?"

"I don't know," I answered honestly.

"Oh," he said. "I understand. I know Amish families don't always stay that close."

"No, that's not it. I don't have a brother."

This fellow just about wrecked the truck in surprise and then blurted out, "Why did you tell Bert you did?"

"I didn't tell Bert," I answered. "He told me."

That Lodi bunch of the Amish aren't quite as bizarre as our Peoli neighbors, but they do take being Swartz-entruber to the limit. The hair is shaggy, the beard long, and the thinking backward. I have more relatives up that way, but I don't admit to that, either.

The thought of me having a look-alike was somewhat exciting. Perhaps some day we'll cross paths and I can pin some of my stunts on him. At the same time, I did manage to catch my reflection in the door mirror. I'd never realized it, but it was sure was time for another haircut.

I hear a lot of folks say they'd like to see an Amish house; they'd like to experience this or try that. In the Plain community, we've got no problem with that as long as folks remember one thing. We're not much on giving things away. We hold to the old, maybe outdated notion that you earn friendships.

Jonas was laid up in the Cleveland hospital for some time a few years back. I'm not sure what the problem was, but the cure was lengthy. While he was up there, he just happened to make friends with Bill, the guy in the next bed.

It may strike you as odd, but this friendship had nothing to do with the fact that Bill or Jonas was different. It began when they discovered they had something in common. They found out that they both liked working with wood. Many a long hour was passed in that hospital room discussing the best way to turn an oak bar on the lathe.

One thing led to another after they both were released,

and Jonas extended the welcome for Bill to come our way. Bill had never married, so maybe it was all the better that he took to Jonas and the family. A visit now and then turned into regular company. Both sides benefited from each visit. Bill would learn about the Plain Peoli, and Jonas was finding that those city people don't bite.

Christmastime came last year, and Bill had made his way to what he was now calling his "adopted" home at Jonas' place. The celebration of our Lord's birth is a festive occasion in our homes, but without those silly decorations. We have no time for the tree or lights, but we don't mind a gift or two.

Gifts were exactly what Bill came toting that day. You should have seen the excitement when the boys discovered that those baseball bats and gloves were for them. The girls cleaned up as well, with so many art and sewing supplies. Jonas got himself a great genealogy book, and Ruth, the lady of the house, was well pleased with the bolt of material and the tub of gourmet popcorn.

Bill was feeling awfully good with all that excitement. Some claim it was the best family feeling he'd ever had. It was so good that he never noticed Jonas Ruth (an Amish way of referring to a man's wife) slip out of the living room and return with a package of her own.

The Amish have to justify the usefulness of a gift before they give it. It was with more than a little tenderness that Ruth said, "We got you this, just in case you come where you belong."

As the paper fell away, Bill couldn't believe it. Jonas and Ruth had been to the buggy makers and bought a lap blanket, in a red tartan, just like theirs. That's family for sure, and I don't think Bill will have much problem remembering that.

Making Amish friends does have a high price, though. If you'd be making friends with the buggy crowd, then you have to put up with some of the world's greatest schemers and connivers. Some claim the Amish are so quiet because they're up to something. One thing for sure: you'd just better be on your toes when you come down the Peoli Road.

Dick is a fellow from Zanesville that's a lot like Bill. He's an Englisher who just took to the Amish. He's been rather good to all of us, but that doesn't mean he's exempt from us taking advantage of him.

It was the morning of the big horse sale down at the county fairgrounds when Dick came driving down the Peoli Road. He pulled into Noah's lane just as Noah was coming out of the back door, putting on his hat and coat.

"Dick, good to see you. I was just going to hitch up and go down to the grocery. Since you're here. . . ."

See what I mean by the scheming? Dick's used to it, so he motioned Noah into the truck. Off they went, Noah chitchatting away like some kid.

They'd almost finished grocery shopping when around the corner came Nelson. That's Noah's little brother, the one still living at home with the old folks.

"Dick, we knew you'd be coming this way. Dad's here, and we were thinking—maybe you could give us a lift and stop by the homeplace?"

More scheming, to be sure. As dearly as Dick loves them all, though, he's not going to be the Guernsey County taxi for the Amish. He begged off, got Noah out of there, and headed back to the house.

When they got back, Noah jumped out and hauled those groceries inside real quick. He came rushing back out and gasped, "Miriam wants you to be here for noon dinner, you know."

"Well, I suppose," Dick teased Noah. "But I might be late. That is, unless you go to that sale with me."

Noah looked at Dick, turned around and ran, not walked, back in the house. In just a second, here he came out the door. In about three strides, Noah was around the truck and inside, ready to go.

It was a good sale, hundreds of head changing hands and several thousand folk to visit with. It might even have been a great sale for Dick—except for Noah. Every fifteen minutes, as regular as a clock himself, Noah would ask Dick what time it was.

This was odd at first, then funny, and it had finally reached the annoying stage by 11:45 p.m. That's when

Noah figured it was time to head home, but he cautioned Dick not to rush it. It was easier to "talk" in a slower-moving vehicle.

Talk Noah did, all the way home. Dick thought his ear was about to fall off. It wouldn't have been so bad, but Noah just seemed to be rambling. Dick did think it strange, but Noah had done peculiar things before.

The Amish aren't anything for that Social Security, taking care of their own elderly. Right next to Noah's place lived his grandmother. As they turned into the lane, Dick couldn't help but notice a couple of buggies at Grandma's hitching post.

"Look there," said Noah shaking his head. "Grandma must have more company again. She'll be ninety-three next year. I sure hope we get company like that when we're old farts like her."

Something about an Amishman calling his grandmother that term hit Dick as being so out of character that it was funny. Dick started laughing, and laughing, and just about getting hysterical. Noah just shrugged it off, jumped out of the truck, trotted up the steps, and disappeared into the house.

When Dick composed himself, he crawled out of the truck, still wiping tears out of his eyes. He was grinning as he climbed the steps and turned the doorknob. When he opened the door, he was hit by the most wondrous smell of dinner.

It was magnificent, the aroma of homemade everything. There was chicken, potatoes, beans, bread, with all the trimmings and extras. It was such a great smell that Dick didn't notice at first that something was wrong. There wasn't any noise in the house, and Noah had six children.

Dick carefully tiptoed through the mudroom, past the kitchen, and peeked around the corner of the living room. There, across the way, stood Noah, Miriam, and the six children, all lined up like steps. Along with them stood Noah's dad (who had been at the store), his mother, brothers, sisters, wives, husbands, and children. One of those CPA types would have counted seventy-six Amish—all together at one time, in one place, because they had to tell Dick some things.

Things like Miriam seeing Dick coming up the road that morning and telling Noah that whatever it took, keep him out of the house. Or that brother Nelson didn't want to go to the auction, nor did his dad. For that matter, neither did Noah. Or the fact that the buggies at the post weren't there visiting Grandma; they were the ones the family didn't have space to hide in the barn.

Maybe it wasn't something Noah's family had to tell Dick, now that I think on it. Maybe it was more something Dick had to be reminded of. They did that the only way they could, singing one of the best renditions of "Happy Birthday" ever heard.

Poor Dick! He'd waited thirty-seven years for a surprise party, and then it was the Amish who threw it.

All of a sudden, that scheming had a purpose!

18

Pranks

What is food to one, is to others bitter poison.
—Lucretius

I've always enjoyed parties like that one for Dick.
Except for one detail, I would have had a grand time last
June when we got together to remind Jake of another year
passing. My cousin Nettie brought along that growth she's
married to.

Calling him a growth is the only label that fits. Grandma Stutzman, who died at ninety-seven, enjoyed every
day of her poor health. This guy doesn't just enjoy the
same unhealth, he relishes every second of misery. Then
he insists on sharing all this grief with the rest of us.

Abe has been sick every time I've seen him since he
married Nettie, and that's been twenty years now. One year
it was terminal gout; the next year the grippe set in. This
year it was the shingles. It was bad enough to hear about
it, but then Abe had to pull up his shirt to show us. Right
there at the table he did this. It was the first time I'd gagged
on food since the rhubarb incident.

Some often wonder if there are certain foods the Amish
don't take to, like those of the Jewish persuasion. For the
most part, every Deutschman I know is on that seafood

diet plan: see food and eat it. Of course, being human beings, there are exceptions to the rule. Jake doesn't like green beans, and Ammon says if his wife fixes potato casserole once more, he'll scream. As for me, it's the rhubarb.

Oh, Sis was growing up those many years ago. She was trying hard to be mother's helper, fixing the meals and graduating on to making pies that one July. That evening after Dad and I came home, she sure did set out a spread.

Sis could cook, and it certainly filled me up. Even at that, there's always room for dessert around an Amish home. Dad sliced a big piece of pie for himself while I took my share as well. It looked delicious, so I launched in with a heaping forkful.

About the time that pie hit my taste buds, I felt my mouth puckering inside out. My eyes started watering and

then rolling around in my head. I thought I might be at the end of my days, especially when I saw Dad peacefully chewing away on his piece.

Those United Nations diplomats could have taken lessons from Dad on glossing over disasters. He got that first piece chewed up and swallowed. There wasn't a tear, a gag, or any other sign of pain as he said, "Carol, you made this pie just the way it ought to be made. You didn't add sugar so I can put in just what I want."

However, I did count it strange that although he was so crazy about the pie, he was standoffish about having the rest of mine. As I recall it now, he always checked to see who made dessert after that. As for me, if I was ever in the wilderness, surrounded by nothing but rhubarb stalks—all I can say is that I'd better get rescued soon.

Just a few weeks after Jake's party, Noah's friend Dick found himself walking a fine line, flirting with disaster. He'd happened by Noah's just as two brand-new, self-propelled lawn mowers were being unloaded from the boxes.

Noah's two oldest boys could hardly wait to see how these beauties would run. Chores may be work to some, but believe it or not, there are others who enjoy a good day's effort. Dick watched the excitement mount before he tossed in a novel thought.

"You know," Dick said. "When I had a self-propelled mower, I had this idea one day. I put a stake in the center of the yard and then tied a rope between the stake and the mower. I just fired it right up, pulled up a chair, and sat there, smoking my pipe and watching the mower going around cutting the whole yard."

They all got a little chuckle out of that before Noah motioned the boys off to work. He waited until the young fellows were out of earshot before he said, "You know they're going to try that."

Dick nodded and said, "Why do you think I mentioned it?"

Probably a month had gone by before Dick was in town again. From a block away, he spied Noah coming for him, waving with both arms to get his attention. As fast as a man can walk, Noah beaded right in on Dick.

"Dick, don't come by the house for a while."

"Why's that, Noah? We're the best of friends."

"True, but the rope broke."

This didn't make a whole of lot of sense to Dick until Noah refreshed his memory.

"The boys tried your trick for cutting the grass, putting a stake out and letting the mower run itself. It worked fairly good the first time. Second time too. Then, during the third try, the rope let go.

"It wouldn't have been so bad, but it let go right as the mower was pointed to Grandma's flower bed. Or what used to be the flower bed.

"She's looking for you, so maybe you should just lie low."

Dick took that advice and steered clear for a good three months. He figured that was plenty of time for things to cool down and memories to fade. He was right for the most part. Grandma only mashed him once with her cane.

Flower gardens like that one are virtually essential to the good Amish homestead. That's Mom's hobby, and she'll make it a real burst of color. For the most part, that just might be the only hobby she does take to.

19

Secret Beauty Treatment

Charm is deceitful, and beauty is vain,
but a woman who fears the Lord is to be praised.
—Proverbs

Beauty is also to be found
in a day's work.
—Mamie Sypert Burns

From time to time, some strangers to the area will rave about how beautiful Amish women tend to be. I cannot argue against that since I hold to the opinion that my wife is the most beautiful girl in the world, and all the rest of the community is finished in a tie for second place. I don't give it much thought. Peoli Road does not exactly have an annual beauty contest. Still, some come looking for the secret of beauty. Just for those curious ones, I investigated and believe I have found that secret Amish recipe.

First would be to rise around 5:30 in the morning to fire up the cookstove. While the potatoes are beginning to fry, start the gasoline washing machine thunking on its first load of laundry for the day. By 6:30 a.m., when the man of the house has eaten and gone off to work, the lady can really indulge in the beauty tricks.

Take that first load of laundry out of the tub and replace it with the second load. Then hang the first load, wet and heavy from the wash, out on a line between the house and the big maple out back. As soon as that wash is hung out, the trick is to grab hold of a hoe as soon as possible and get into the garden to start thinning out the weeds before the day is hot.

The beauty treatment continues right through hanging out the second load of wash and a quick lunch. Then carefully harness the buggy horse, attach the shafts to the rigging, and head over to the neighbors for putting in a quilt. Three hours there of vigorously exercising both fingers and gums does wonders for the soul.

By this time, as the sun begins to decline, go back home, take in the wash, fold some, and make another pile to be pressed in another basket. Be sure to get a huge supper on the stove, timed to be ready to eat within a minute of when the husband comes home.

Being such a comprehensive beauty treatment, it can't be too surprising to learn that the remedy continues on after supper. Be sure to wash the dishes spotless, and then get the ironing done. With a touch of luck, there's just enough time to get a few chapters read in the Good Book before it's time to put out the light and curl into bed.

Not what the average beauty book tells you? That could be, but I've never read one. I'll stand by my earlier statement, though. That's the way she spent the day, and Mrs. Beachy is, and always will be, beautiful.

All in all, down our road you're going to find a pretty good bunch of mothers, housekeepers, and seamstresses. I would like to be able to tell you what makes Nettie such a good cook or why Ruth can stitch so nice, but I always get run off before I can find out. The kitchen and the sewing room are Mom's kingdom, and the menfolk are not to get underfoot.

It is not true that such things as quilting bees are strictly for fun. I heard some tourists talking once in Winesburg about those poor Amish women. They were saying—proving how dumb they were more than anything else—that the women's only amusement was gabbing at a quilting. I grant that there's a great deal of socializing going on, but that quilt is being put in to be used. We all remember how cold it got a few years back, and those quilts felt really good right then. Come to think of it, that was the cold stretch nine months before the baby boom around here.

Thinking about hobbies carries over to the men as well. Many of the Amish like to work with wood. It's not that they want to hang out a shingle for the tourist, but you never can tell when another piece of furniture might be necessary. Marvin was three legs done on a high chair before he realized why his wife might be asking for such an item.

I'm not saying that furniture needs are all that great at home. Pop will have an overstuffed chair for himself, and Mom will have a smaller version. Maybe a nice couch and some straight-backed chairs will fill out the rest of the seating needs. Of course, there's a dining room table and chairs in the farm kitchen, too, but perhaps it's more noticeable what the Amish do without.

You'll not find the carpet man getting much business with the Plain People. A throw rug, rag or hooked, does nicely. They are not much for decorations, either, other than a calendar or two and maybe a few religious sayings carved on plaques. Pretty simple, going along with a simple life.

Even the heat and lights tend to run to the simple back home. Remember, we don't go for electricity. Our hillbilly neighbors heat with wood and read by candle, oil lamp, or lantern. But most of us now let propane take care of all that.

Yep, it's a simple life. It probably would be a lot simpler if there wasn't the rest of the world. You try to walk the straight and narrow, but then things of the world jump right out in front of you. Take what happened to Jake's cousin Levi.

Levi doesn't live around here. He has a farm a lot further north, up east of Cleveland. Levi farms and is a faithful sort, but he's also somewhat curious about the city of Cleveland itself.

A while back, Levi talked his neighbor, an Englishman, into giving him a ride into town. It seems this Englisher works there someplace. Off they went one morning, one to work and the other just to look around.

Five o'clock came, and Levi met his friend. He had a good day, didn't see all that much that was so great, but he did appreciate the lift. They made their way home, and the Englishman didn't think anymore about it. At least not until the evening news came out.

The lead story that night on the local news was that the police had raided one of those houses of ill repute. They had film on the cops leading people out of this building. Then they panned over the crowd of spectators.

It was a rough-looking crowd, but it was the roughest side of town. A real sin city. Maybe to some there wasn't any as rough looking as the guy standing right in the middle of the front row of spectators. The one with the long black hair, the beard, and the black felt hat. The one named Levi.

The outside world also causes excitement with its statewide lottery. Not too many weeks back, the pot grew to more millions than one can count. I'm not for that, nor are other Plain People, for it's gambling. But, if somebody else would win and share the benefit, that's worth thinking about.

Thinking about it we were, down at the mill one rainy Thursday when driver Joe was ready to divide up money he never won. He wanted to know, though, if he really won, what we'd all want.

Freeman thought about it and then said, "I always wanted to be a farmer, but I'm not greedy. You can get me the farm this year. Next year, with the next check, you can get me the cows."

We got a laugh out of that. Then Joe turned to Ivan, Freeman's brother, and asked him what he'd want.

Without a second's thought, Ivan says, "A Cadillac."

Such a statement was like dropping a bomb on all of us, for Ivan is a pillar of the church. All his life Ivan has been buggy-bound. Here he was, shaking us all up by saying such a thing. But he wasn't done.

"Not any Cadillac," he went on. "A big one. One I can drive around in. One I can put those big whitewalls on and the fuzzy stuff on the dash. Then I'll put a big Scorpio decal on the rear window. Last, but not least, I'll trade my church hat for one of those purple ones with a white feather in it.

"Just think—the Amish pimp."

It seems that somebody else had been to the big city more than he admitted to, but I'm not naming names.

20

Trouble Creeps In

As a stake is driven firmly into a fissure between stones,
so sin is wedged in between selling and buying.
—Sirach

A well-adjusted person is one who
makes the same mistake twice
without getting nervous.
—Jane Heard

Just a few months ago, I heard some distressing news about the affairs of the world. A United States congressman from Ohio was relieved of his elected position. According to the story we picked up, this fellow got into an elevator there in the House and couldn't keep his hands off the young lady who was running the thing.

As I reflect on this, it disturbs me a great deal. I feel bad that a man would have such a weakness and hope he receives treatment as soon as possible. I feel worse for the young lady, one who is entitled to her own space and privacy. What I find most aggravating, though, is the whole situation our country finds itself in.

I suppose I should be glad we're not for the notion of running for public office. Can you imagine all these representatives from all over the United States, looking out for our best interests, and they're too dumb to run an elevator by themselves? I had that figured out about the first time I was ever in the thing, but I'm not saying anything about my savvy. We've got a senator coming up for reelection, and I'd hate for folks to think I might be about as smart as he is.

Once in a while, not often, but on occasion, maybe the Amish do initiate a few problems of their own. Everybody is trying to lead a solid life, but humanity does creep in. It's not that we go looking for trouble, but it does find some of us.

There was a fellow who went up from the Peoli Road to Sugarcreek. He shopped around a bit before he came across a clothing store. Tucked away in the back, this place had a whole selection of Amish straw hats. There

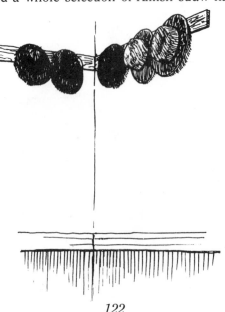

were hats for most of those twelve styles of Amish people I mentioned earlier.

This was an absolute bonanza for the fellow, because collecting hats was his hobby. True, even though he was loyal to one faction, he had collected representative hats worn by just about every faction. The one hat missing in his collection was the rounded crown and wider brim of the Andy Weaver bunch. Sure enough, in front row center, there it was.

The hat was purchased in a blink, and off this fellow went. It just happened to be a bright, sunny day, so he figured he'd give this new hat a test drive. He put his old hat in the bag, put the new one on, and strolled up to the corner.

Just as he reached that corner, a buggy pulled up to the traffic light. Naturally, with this fellow's luck, the young ladies on board were of the local Andy Weaver congregation. They looked over, recognized that the fellow sporting the Andy Weaver hat was not one of their own, and proceeded to toss their heads in righteous indignation.

When this didn't have the desired effect of making the fellow slink away in guilt, the young lady holding the lines took the next step of disapproval. She scowled a death glare at him, who just happened to be me.

It could be that I've been around too many English people, or maybe I just wasn't thinking. Considering the scene, I did what came natural: I stuck my tongue out.

Before I could realize what I'd done, making this horrible gesture at those pious girls, they both had their tongues out at me. They pulled away in a huff, sure this impostor was insane. As for me, I was sitting on the curb laughing my head off at how worldly those not of the world can be.

Earlier this year I got into a mess that maybe was not as bad, or maybe was worse. A friend, an Englisher, was a big shot with the American Red Cross over northwest of here. One June day he came driving up our lane.

I told Henry it was a little early for the blood drive, but that wasn't it. His chapter of the Red Cross had a project. A poor family in his area had a fire and nothing but bad luck since. The Red Cross set their caps to it and found a church to fund the supplies. Then one of the wise ones went to his neighbors and rounded up a work crew. It was because of this work crew that I fit into the equation.

The workers were Amish of Henry's area, a little more liberal than around here, and all were farmers. There was not a carpenter among them. Henry had come looking for a boss, someone to estimate the project and ramrod it through to the end. It took me about three minutes to get my tools and a few clothes, and off we went.

I don't get to Henry's home much, it being way too far by the buggy. Maybe the car is more convenient, covering in two hours what would take me three days, but we don't need such a thing for our own use. It was good to visit at his place, though, before we headed out to the project.

In around twenty minutes I had it figured out. It worried me that the job was looking so simple. I put the tape on everything again. They called in my list to the lumberyard, and we headed off to Henry's to wait for the morning and get this one done.

We got on the job about eight that next morning. The lumberyard had already delivered the materials, and it wasn't but fifteen minutes before a van came down the street carrying the work crew. They piled out, chatted a bit, had me divvy up the job, and the work began.

These boys might be farmers for a living, but they did a good impression of carpenters that day. They worked hard, and they did things the way I wanted. I wasn't having a single problem until about ten that morning.

That's when one of the farmers came over and mentioned that we were running a little short on two-by-fours. About twenty short, in fact. That might not have bothered me, since anybody can make a mistake, but an hour later we were two hundred feet short of pine board.

I was smelling fish without an ocean nearby. Sure enough, just before dinner, one of the younger Amish fellows I'd been friendly with stopped to visit a bit.

After some of this and that, he said, "Say, when the project's over, you take all the excess home with you for your crew, don't you?"

I just shook my head, knowing what was coming next.

"Oh," he went on, "then maybe we could make you a good price on what's left over?"

We held a meeting right after dinner that day. There weren't any raised voices or threats, nothing like that. Only firm words. I don't know who planned on building what that day, but it never happened. By the time the day ended, the project was done, and every farmer's eyes were on his shoes whenever I looked at them. It just happened that we managed to have twenty two-by-fours and two hundred feet of pine stock left over. Really can't begrudge a good try, though.

Far be it from me to be too critical of those fellows, considering what happened up in Holmes County two months back. I didn't start the trouble, but—well, maybe I'd just better explain.

I'd gone visiting to Cousin Jake's for the weekend.

When some unexpected company arrived to spend the day, we decided we'd slip on down to one of those cheese factories and pick up some samples for nibbling food. Jake and I hitched up the buggy and headed off. This gave me a chance to find out more about his unusual visitors.

The guests were some of Ohio's New Order Amish, a bunch that separated from the Old Order around 1967-69. I'd seen their kind of buggies before, with sliding doors and rubber-rimmed wheels, but I'd never had a chance to see some up close before. Different, to say the least, but I'm not saying there's all that much wrong with that, either.

The women seem to like the brighter colors, still plain pattern dresses, but lighter hues than we see around Peoli. Also, the girls aren't above having an opinion of their own, I might note. If more of Holmes County took to this concept, there might be a little less of "the old man's word is law" thinking before long.

The fellows were different, too, especially in having English haircuts. For me to get a trim, all that's required is a bowl and the shears. The upside-down bowl on the head guides the clipping. These fellows had the hair cut around the ears, nice and neat. The beards were shorter, too, and one fellow even said he wasn't growing one until he married. This was unusual for Ohio, where we've always worn whiskers as soon as they'd grow after baptism.

What I found really unusual was that the New Orders have church every other Sunday, like we do, but then have Sunday school on the off Sundays. The young people have Wednesday night fellowship as well, a novel idea to me. Since this family seemed to be so fine, there must be something to this sort of thinking.

I complimented Jake on his choice of friends and commented on how little I knew about this New Order. We began talking about all those Amish factions, feeling sorry that some sociologist, anthropologist, or another ologist didn't put out a book on the subject. We figured that, should the author split enough hairs, as those who are book-learning smart tend to do, this text should be about the size of an encyclopedia.

Jake was saying he'd read the Amish population was growing about six percent each year. Even with migration or losing some to the world, our people expect to be near one hundred thousand strong in this state alone in my lifetime. Maybe someday all folks would have daily contact with the Amish, and we wouldn't be such a tourist novelty. Such an encyclopedia just might have some value, but it will take a smart one to write it. That sure lets out everybody I know.

At any rate, we got down there to the cheese place, and you should have seen the tourists. Fourteen busloads we counted, and the cars too, all there to buy cow by-products, as Jake calls it. We got in line with the rest of them, made our selection, and shuffled over to the counter.

Just as I put the cheese on the scale, the girl running the place asked, "Do you ship your milk here?"

I was going to say no when I felt Jake's size twelve pressing on top of my size sevens. More out of pain than anything, I nodded.

"All right," she said, "what's your name?"

I looked at Jake, and his look back meant, I should tell her my name. I figured I'd better play this one pretty safe, using the Amish equivalent of John Smith.

"It's Mose Yoder," I replied.

Jake did keep a straight face while the girl got out her

list. She ran down through it and then looked up all confused.

"There's sixteen Mose Yoders on this list. Which one are you?"

Jake leaned over, acting like he was checking the list, and said, "I think he's the second one here."

Yes, it's forgery, theft, fraud, and just about every other crime known to man, all for 25 percent off. I know it, and I felt bad about it. Bad enough to say something, but only outside the cheesery.

I tapped Jake and said, "What did you make me do that for?"

Jake shook his head and said, "I'm not the one saying my name is Mose Yoder."

Since I was taking all the guilt, I wouldn't have felt so bad if I'd gotten all the cheese. It didn't come out that way. Jake ate his share plus some. He ate so much that he wanted me to go back with him and buy some more.

Can you believe it? Larceny! And then he wants me to be a part of it again. I can just tell you one thing. It worked the second time, too.

It's really not far off to claim that Mose Yoder down home is just like John Smith in Cleveland or Columbus. The Amish have a limited number of last names, and Yoder is probably most common. Then there are Miller, Weaver, Troyer, Stutzman, Schlabach, Hershberger, and a few others that include Beachy.

First names aren't much more numerous. The Amish are partial to biblical names, and Moses leads the pack again. Down home, just like in most Amish communities, it's not at all unusual to find six Mose Yoders, all on the same road.

The worldly types likely don't see any problem, figuring that everybody then goes by their middle name. Well, that is precisely the problem: with the exception of the New Order crowd, the Amish don't have middle names.

Dad is Roy, so my middle initial is R. He's Amos's boy, so Pop is Roy A. The middle name is actually an initial, the first initial of your father's first name, boys and girls alike. But don't worry about any confusion. The Amish figured out a solution years ago, and that's precisely why they invented nicknames.

Sure enough, Hardware Mose works in the store selling nails, while Potato Mose grows the spuds down on the farm. It's a custom that carries over everywhere, whether your name is common or not. All it takes is for you to get your foot, or your fork, caught in your mouth.

"That's the dumbest thing I ever saw," Sam said, looking right at me.

"What?" I answered. "You sure ate more than I did."

"Not that. But the spuds. Four helpings, and you didn't eat no gravy."

I've always thought that was the only way to eat mashed potatoes. I never cared for the watery stuff they call gravy. Now, even if I wanted to, there's no way I can enjoy the sauce.

If you come our direction asking for Eli, you'll be headed off in four directions. Ask for the Beachy place, and there's five possibilities. Ask for No Gravy, and they'll tell you exactly where I can be found.

21

The Target

These objects . . . were of eternal importance, like baseball.
—Sinclair Lewis

*If people concentrated on the really important things in
life, there'd be a shortage of fishing poles.*
—Doug Larson

I saw Woody Hershberger the other day. That probably
doesn't mean anything to you, but around here Woody is a
living legend. Woody's not his real name, but none of us
would have been keen on being called Joshua, either.
What is real, though, is Woody's claim to immortality.

Thirty years ago Woody decided he was going to have
the world's fastest bicycle. To achieve all that speed, he
knew he had to make the cycle lighter. Therefore, the first
thing he took off was the brakes.

Nobody ever claimed Woody was a genius, but it went
downhill from there. Literally downhill, right to the bottom
of the steepest decline in the county, Peoli Ridge Road.
When Ervin and I got there on our bikes, Woody was just
starting down the hill.

Credit must be given to Woody, for neither Ervin nor I
had ever seen anybody ride that fast. He was going a blue
streak. About the time we really appreciated how fast he

was going, Woody was beginning to realize the first of two problems.

When you come to the bottom of Peoli Ridge Road, you have to turn. It's either left or right onto Valley Road, but not straight. Not yet, at least. About the time Woody realized he'd have to make a decision, he caught sight of the second problem. The entire foot of that decline was covered with gravel. Whichever way he went, he was assured of a fall and at least a broken bone or two.

Much to our surprise, the inventive Woody created a third option when he came to the bottom of that hill. He went straight. Straight into the concrete bridge on the far side of the road.

To this day, I can still see that bike stop dead and Woody doing a perfect one-and-a-half somersault into the creek. He no more than hit the water than we saw a fishing pole thrown up into the air, heard Bobby Troyer scream, and saw him take off running.

We rushed down to the bridge in terror. Troyer was still running, out of sight by now. As we looked over the railing, there lay Woody right beside Bobby's tackle box. He had a glazed-over look in his eyes, having apparently missed Bobby by no more than a foot when he came flying in from outer space.

Although I was only ten years old, I'd say we handled the emergency quite well. Ervin and I dragged Woody out of the creek, laid him over the frame of his bicycle like the Indians put their dead on a pony, and walked him home. We dumped him at his back door, knocked twice, and then ran like Bobby Troyer.

Woody recovered his health, but he never was the same. When he got to be of age, he ended up marrying one of those Swartzentruber girls. That was fifteen children ago, and she's expecting again. Even if he wouldn't have gone over the bridge, he'd probably have that glazed look in his eyes, all things considered.

Whether it is No Gravy or Mose Yoder, I'll need an alias should my next adventure turn out not so well. Levi, Jake, Ammon, and I are conspiring to steal a barn. Not the whole barn, just the back wall of it. What we're going to do with it after that is beyond us right now—but we want to do something. After all, that wall is just about sacred.

This treasure is only a few miles southwest, standing on a Swartzentruber farm. It's just another barn to the old hillbilly who lives there. For the life of him, he can't figure out what's so interesting about a wall that's got a nice big bullseye carved on it.

According to the story, the family who owned the place before the Amish were good folk. Good, except that one son was nothing for farm work. It doesn't cut any ice with the Swartzentrubers that the young fellow would rather throw rocks at this target he'd carved on the barn wall than plow or do his choring.

It doesn't matter to the hillbilly that the boy, Denton by name, became good enough by throwing the rocks to try throwing baseballs over in Newcomerstown. Once he started doing that, he wasn't anything at all for the farm work. Then it wasn't too long before Denton left the area altogether.

This Swartzentruber's parents bought the place a few years later. The Amishman, an old man now, has lived his entire life on the grounds, never knowing what happened to worthless Denton.

Levi and I know, though. We've read enough and heard

enough to know that Denton did play ball for Newcomerstown. He did well, good enough to take a chance. Denton borrowed some money, bought a suit of clothes, and took a trip up to Cleveland.

All those rocks thrown at that barn wall must have had some value. Once Denton got a chance, major league baseball never saw a ball thrown so fast. As fast a cyclone, in fact.

Denton the cyclone. Denton Cyclone Young. Cy Young, the winningest pitcher in baseball history. And it all started a few miles from right here. I've never seen one of those big-time ball games, but I'd like to have that target! There's just something about a memory, however you care to imagine it, that's wonderful.

We never knew about the barn until we were talking to a highway patrolman a few years back. Walter had seen us playing ball at the school one Saturday and thought we might like the story. It was a good one, but so was Walter.

Walt was a big ox in that gray uniform. He just looked like he wouldn't take lip from anybody. I think the whole county was afraid of him for about a week. Then we found out the biggest thing about him was his heart.

More than one night Walt would follow an Amish teenager, a little deep in the jug, all the way home. He'd keep his lights flashing the whole way, taking care of what he called "my boys." It was no happy day when Walt was transferred on to another post.

It was even a sadder day last January when news came through the mail that Walt had passed away. He'd suffered with cancer, even when he was here, yet never shared a moment's pain. It was something that needed to be thought out. There was no better man, unless it's my dad.

22

Paradise

An asylum of the sane.
—Anonymous

*The fewer the facts,
the stronger the opinion.*
— Arnold H. Glasow

I spent most of an hour on top of the hill behind the house. It's my place to be alone, think on things, and air some things out. The hilltop is my private place to regret all the things I never said until it was too late. It was drizzling a bit, but I never felt it as I looked to the north, out over Troyer's farm.

I take great stock in the fact that in our Father's house are many mansions. I don't want to be putting words in our Lord's mouth or stepping out of line, but standing up there surveying the valley sure can make a person hope. Looking over Troyer's place made me hope all the more.

The way I'm wishing, when that day comes where one life ends and another begins, I'll be lucky enough to find myself heading up a long gravel lane. If you'd bear to the right, up the hill, you'd head to the house. The women will be there, Grandma and the rest, doing this and that. I'll be

there before long to do some visiting, but there's some business first.

The lane bends left to the barn, right through the playground. Mary's Miriam is there, her suffering over now. The twins, too, the ones who never had a chance to feel the love that Momma and I saved just for them. I'll linger, but only for a moment.

It's to the far side of the barn that I'm headed. Over to the shady side, under the overhang. That's where you'll find the long, low bench. Grandpa is already there, along with Unc, Daniel's dad too, and Walt just taking a seat. I can almost hear them saying, "Good to see you, boy. Sit down, rest for eternity, and tell us the one about...."

The sound of my name being called brought me back to reality. I turned around and looked at the house. The girl I married last April 2 was waving me down the hill for supper. With my idea of the afterlife gone for the moment and a smile on my face, I headed down to the woman of my dreams.

How exciting it is to wait for tomorrow in this paradise we live in today. How thrilling to dream of the paradise our Lord has made for us, knowing how beautiful it will be. With that to carry along in our heart every day, sometimes it's hard to be sad.

If we assume that I started thinking somewhat like an adult when I finished school at age fourteen, that's given me twenty-six years of deliberate thought to get everything figured out. Well, I haven't. I don't even have one single thing figured. As it stands right now, I'm still stuck on the first issue I even considered.

It strikes me peculiar that the people of Ohio, even with 180 years of practice, can't get used to the Amish. The Plain People aren't saints, not mystic seers of another world, nor some secret society cloistered away from the world. That first Amish farm was cleared near Walnut Creek in 1809. Since then, the Plain People remain what they've always been — just plain people.

I've read that there was another bunch of people in Ohio long before the Amish. Nobody understood them, either, nor did they try to from what I can see. Instead, these different ones were lumped into one big category, even though there were different tribes of them, too. One faction even called themselves Our People, just like us. With their own language, dress, and customs, they tried hard to be a people apart. It was easy to call them all "the Indians." Just like hanging a label on all of us, "the Amish."

Unlike the Native Americans, the Amish know exactly what is happening to them. Land development will take more farmland this year, turning it into housing developments. Tourists will keep coming, buying from foreign hucksters, and never notice that their car or bus is breaking up another section of roadway. Self-appointed experts will continue to perpetrate misinformation until all hope of understanding is gone. If we continue to take, and take, and take from any resource, natural or human, without giving back, we won't have much that is worth saving before too long.

We know some Amish will cut their hair and go into the world, never to return. More still will leave, going off to Amish Wisconsin or Amish Kentucky to be left alone, if only for a few more years. All because nobody much listens anymore, all too happy living in bliss. After all, isn't that what ignorance is?

The loafers at the mill talk often of what Wisconsin must be like. When asked if I'd consider moving to such a place, I answered that I didn't plan on it. I know all too well that we cannot figure what the next sunrise might bring, but for now we will stay right here.

We were born Amish and will die the same. It is the only life we know. Our life, our way, our people. Forever trapped in a community which a man once described as "an asylum of the sane." Backward by choice, we carry on until perhaps those of the world slow down enough to catch up to us.

If there's been one thing I've wanted to get across in our visit, it's that the Amish are people. Of all the other things so many talk about—weddings, funerals, why we're not so keen on photos, or whatever—the only point is that the Peoli Road is made up of people, not animals in a zoo or circus freaks. Sometimes we forget, but being real people, there's real vice even in the Plain People.

Tobacco has a market among the Plain People, smoking and chewing the leaf alike. Around the homeplace, the rule was that if I'd refrain from chewing until my eighteenth birthday, Grandpa's gold pocket clock would be mine. I'm pleased to report that I achieved that objective, and that timepiece is now ticking in my pocket. Actually, the chew never was for me. I might note, though, before some think wrong, that nobody ever said anything about not learning to smoke a pipe.

Even seeing the many smokers in those buggies, there must be twice as many who indulge in another vice. Grandma Beachy at the age of ninety-four did not need glasses. No, sir, she drank it right out of the bottle. It's sad that some Amish imbibe a bit too much. Some end up in Alcoholic Anonymous. Others are like Isaac. He's the best barn builder in Ohio, but he's only working six months a year now. The other six, he's stewed to the gills. I'm not one to say it's a sickness, but it sure is a problem.

There is one other vice common among the Amish men, but I don't see it as much of a problem. This failing is unexpected, but that's the fault of the rest of the world for equating *Amish* and *angel*. The next time you're to a horse sale and spot a crowd of fellows all huddled around, it could be they're discussing business. More than likely, though, somebody is in the process of telling what we call a *schmutzich* story.

For example: There was this boy, and his name was Marvin. When Marvin was two, his dad died. Around the age of five, Marvin began noticing that there were boys and there were girls in the world.

Marvin went to his mother and said, "Maw, how does the doctor tell the difference between a baby boy and a baby girl?"

Well, Marvin's mother is a sharp one, and she said. . . .

There may be women reading this, so this saga of Marvin, a real blue corker, doesn't need to go any further. Should any of you fellows happen by the sale barn some time, though, be sure to look me up. You might find out why this is an all-time favorite.

One I probably could tell you was the story I caught wind of when I was up to Bontrager's buggy shop last week. I had a creeper wheel on the hack that didn't have many miles left on it. I stopped by to pick up a new one, and like most visits up that way, time just slipped away.

Bontrager is always glad to see me coming and cuts me a good price. I'd suppose he's still being grateful to me for giving him the good price when I sold him the business some years back. It had been my uncle Lester's until he died in a home accident. I took over for the next few years, putting to use all I knew. It was a good business, but all things considered, carpentering seemed more appealing.

We talked about Lester while I was there. With all the medicines around today, the doctors probably could have brought his epilepsy under control. Maybe he wouldn't have killed himself, and maybe he still would have done it. Those weren't real good times, him being sick and my folks leaving the valley for the uptown. Thinking back on it, I can honestly say the best thing about those days is that they're over.

At any rate, from what Bontrager was saying, there was a certain Swartzentruber family. You could tell they hadn't been married long, for they only had seven children, all boys. Well, things went pretty well on the farm one year, and they decided they'd all go out to eat one day.

They drove down to the Salt Fork Lodge, went in, and no more than sat down when the little one, Amos, said he had to go to the bathroom.

His mother asked if he could find it. He thought so, and off he went. In a few minutes he was back.

"Well," Mom said, "did you find it?"

"No."

She sent the next oldest. They came back, and they hadn't found it. She sent three, four, five, and then six of them. Each time they came back, not having found it. Finally, she sent all seven boys.

Well, the boys stayed and stayed and stayed. Finally, after what seemed like an eternity, here they all came. Right over to the table, and sat right down.

"Did you find it?" Mom asked.

"Finally," answered the oldest one, Junior.

Mom said, "All right, I saw other people get up, go out, and then come back like they'd been to the restroom. They didn't seem to have any problems. What was your problem?"

"No real problem, Mom," Junior said. "Amos just had his pants on backwards."

23

Life Goes On

A time to be born, and a time to die.
—Ecclesiastes

I was thinking on that Swartzentruber story just a week ago Thursday as I came walking down the Peoli Road. Levis had gone to see family up in Wisconsin, and I was choring for them. It was probably nine o'clock by the time I had everything squared away that morning, though it was raining pretty good and you couldn't tell from the sun.

As I rounded the bend, here came Old Weaver, headed up to the harness shop for some rigging repairs. We paused on the road to visit. I shared that tale about little Amos with him, and we had quite a laugh. We chatted a bit, about nothing really, before we went our separate ways.

As my memory serves me, I was just going up the front steps when the car went by. Sure, he was going quick, but I've seen them quicker. Anyway, nine in the morning is too early to be drinking.

Some say the fellow in the car never saw Weaver's rig. Most figure Weaver never felt a thing. The only thing that's for sure now is that Weaver is dead.

We bear the drunk no grudge; that's not our way. Still, it gave me something to think about as I listened to a funeral being preached for four hours at the homeplace.

We wouldn't wish Weaver back. With God's blessing, he'll find his paradise. Still, it gave me even more to think on as I dug my friend's grave and then covered it over for eternity.

We had more than enough to go through on that day as the sun began its decline. It was an hour or so before dark when half a dozen of us congregated down at the mill. It was crisp, but not yet winter cold.

The crowd that had collected likes to consider ourselves the trustees of the Peoli Road, the wise ones and all, but the womenfolk much prefer to brand us for what we are—the loafers. At any rate, we were all standing there, sipping on a little of the homemade root beer Mose likes to brew up when all of a sudden, running down the road, here came Samuel. He was running so fast I was afraid the house was on fire.

"No, no," he managed to gasp out, "it's my wife. The little one's on the way!"

Those somber faces of the loafers started to turn to smiles as we watched Samuel dash to the telephone booth to call Joe, a local fellow who likes to drive for the Amish. Those smiles broadened into grins by the time the old blue Ford pickup came rushing into town.

The thought of such a joyous occasion as a new arrival in our community called for another round of the root beer as we watched Samuel hop into that truck and head off down Old 21, headed for Memorial Hospital. We were but three or four sips into the mug where here came Joe, racing up the road past us and right on up the Peoli Road.

We were still laughing when Joe came back through town, this time blowing the air horn and hooting and hollering out the window. It was the best reminder we could have had, seeing Samuel trying to make himself invisible in the cab of that truck beside his wife.

For everyone who goes, another will take his place. For one more day, life goes on, even down the Peoli Road.

• • •

Life did go on, down the Peoli Road. It was just a few weeks after Old Weaver's funeral that the flu bug passed through. I had no more than recovered from that when an accident at work unexpectedly changed an entire lifestyle.

Time was on my hands while recuperating, and I found myself at an auction one November Saturday. With a single nod of my head, I retired from carpentering to life on the farm.

It will be an adventure, to say the least, but there's nowhere I'd rather be. Why, there's even a large slice of humble pie to be eaten. I've discovered that my new neighbors, soon to be friends, are, of all things, Swartzentruber.

Coming after the harvest of 1992, *Stories from the Farm* plans on capturing it all. Hope to see you there.

Yours,

Eli

Eli

The Author

It's been forty years since a little woodchopper named Eli arrived at the Beachy home overlooking the Peoli Valley. From a simple beginning, his simple life evolved in the Plain world. He was raised near Newcomerstown, Ohio, in the southeast corner of the largest concentration of Amish in the world.

Armed with a basic Amish education, Beachy became a buggymaker in his earlier years. Even then, Eli was always one who could take a bit of news, stretch it this way and that, and end up with a story fit for entertaining company in the evenings.

The buggy shop changed hands, and Beachy followed his father into a career in carpenter work. Then he found something else more important, that essential of life known as his wife, Sharon. Never blessed with children, Beachy and his wife make their home in Wayne County, Ohio. They are members of a local Amish congregation.

Beachy also writes a column for a local newspaper and tells tales like these to groups interested in the Amish.

In a world of convenience and perpetual change, three things are sure. There'll always be Amish, they won't always make sense, and most importantly, there'll always be one more story to tell, especially along the Peoli Road.